LONDON
CONTEMPORARY
DANCE
THEATRE

◆

THE FIRST 21 YEARS

LONDON CONTEMPORARY DANCE THEATRE

◆

THE FIRST 21 YEARS

TEXT BY MARY CLARKE AND CLEMENT CRISP

PHOTOGRAPHS BY ANTHONY CRICKMAY

DANCE BOOKS CECIL COURT LONDON

For Robin Howard, Robert Cohan and Janet Eager

ACKNOWLEDGEMENTS

This book could not have been written without the tireless research, the know-ledge and understanding of Angela Kane, whose work in the Contemporary Dance Trust's archives has produced all the material we have used. We are immensely grateful to her. We must also thank Sue Merrett for undertaking the formidable task of compiling the index.

We must also express our gratitude to the staff at The Place, who so kindly helped Miss Kane, and offer our personal thanks to Robin Howard, to Robert Cohan and to Janet Eager, to Patricia Hutchinson Mackenzie and to Dr Richard Ralph, who all contributed reminiscences and information that have proved essential in our task.

To Anthony Crickmay, all gratitude for the photographs which contribute so much to this record.

MC/CC, London 1987

First published in 1989 by Dance Books Ltd.,
9 Cecil Court, London WC2N 4EZ.
ISBN 185273 002 1

Text © 1989 Mary Clarke & Clement Crisp
Photographs © 1989 Anthony Crickmay
Edited by Kathy Elgin
Designed by Paul Bowden

Distributed in the USA by Princeton Book Co.,
P.O. Box 109, Pennington, N.J. 08542.
Printed by BAS Printers, Over Wallop, Hampshire.

British Library Cataloguing in Publication Data
Clarke, Mary, 1923–
London Contemporary Dance Theatre.
1. London. Dance theatres. London Contemporary Dance Theatre
I. Title
793.3′09421

ISBN 1-85273-002-1

Frontispiece and front cover: Anthony van Laast and Patrick Harding-Irmer, photographed in rehearsal by Anthony Crickmay.

The photographs in this book are by Anthony Crickmay with the exception of the following: p.55 (Frederika Davis); pp.58, 71 (Colin Clark); p.64 (Helen Leoussi); pp.106, 178, 187 (Bill Cooper); p.105 (BBC); pp.159, 163, 167, 172, 188 (David Buckland); p.185 (Dee Conway).

CONTENTS

◆

FOREWORD

by Robert Cohan

◆

When Robin Howard invited me to London twenty-one years ago, his brief to me was 'to bring an injection of American contemporary dance to Britain' and 'to form a dance company based on love'. An unashamedly ideal idea, perhaps. I was not sure it was possible. Performing dance in Britain was synonymous with ballet for most of the population for many years. How could we find an audience for modern dance – how could we even find theatres that would present us? Many theatre managers thought we were a ballroom dance company.

The audience – and many critics – were not used to seeing bare feet on stage, and after generations of western societies trying to get off the floor and onto elegant chairs, here were people crawling around on the floor again. Many people found our movement too offensive to their ideas of proper dance. We were also bringing a different language; one in which the entire body spoke the meaning of the dance in a complicated and abstract way. It was acceptable if it was in a dance that had a surface of visual and rhythmic excitement, but not if it was in a dance that was intensely dramatic and serious. All of these conditions for the reception of our work we had to try to change. Our methods were mostly hard work – training dancers until their bodies became finely tuned explicit instruments, and trying to explain our art to everyone we could possibly reach through lecture demonstrations, residencies and teaching.

The other part of my brief, to build a professional dance company based on love, appeared more difficult. I came from twenty-one years' hard training in the intensely competitive dance schools of New York City. Love was for after working hours (your family) or in an abstract way for your art, not something to bind a dance company together.

I remembered the best piece of advice I have ever been given about teaching. You must teach only what you know, and that must mean everything you know, and you must give all that hard-earned knowledge generously and with love. That way you will grow as a teacher because the act of emptying yourself will allow you to be refilled by your students' understanding. I tried to put that principle into practice here. I had to change to do it but it was made easier by the extraordinary people who gravitated to work at The Place over the years.

I can't claim that I know enough about love to say that it worked but I can claim that we have almost always had a happy and dedicated company of extraordinary dancers. The quality of 'a kind of love' that the company projects from the stage is certainly a large part of our popularity and success.

Patrick Harding-Irmer in Robert Cohan's Class *(1975). Photograph by Bill Cooper*

I think Robin and I have accomplished most of what we set out to do in these twenty-one years. There is a thriving dance scene in Britain of both performers and audience. The level of teaching of contemporary dance is so high that now dancers trained here are working all over the world.

We must all thank Robin Howard for having the imagination to see that all this could happen in the first place – and then, in those financial crises that seemed to loom every year, for his consistently finding the money for us to keep going until he didn't have any more to give. We also must thank all of the people who worked at The Place all these years because they not only gave fully of themselves in their jobs but they did so, and are still doing so, for salaries so low that they are directly supporting the arts as much as the arts-funding bodies are.

The story of Contemporary Dance Trust is like an adventure story; a story that starts with an idea for an expedition into the unknown; a journey along a perilous road, battles fought – some lost but most won. But, unlike real adventure stories, it still has no ending; just a pause to celebrate twenty-one years of survival and perhaps to climb a tree to get a glimpse of the terrain ahead.

1987

INTRODUCTION

◆

This book is very specifically about one enterprise, the Contemporary Dance Trust and all its related activities – the school which is at the heart of everything it does, the company which has so exultantly implanted a contemporary dance style into the everyday life of the nation, and the various educational and community projects which are so important a part of the Trust's work. It grew, as we shall show, from the idealism, love and hope born in one man, Robin Howard, during the first visit to London of the Martha Graham company in 1954. Howard it was who had the foresight to persuade Robert Cohan to join him in what must have seemed a gigantic task, and the faith to continue by never letting go the standards of excellence which he and Cohan had set from the very beginning. But before embarking on this chronicle we must make brief reference to Graham's predecessors in bringing 'modern dance' to Britain and establishing a then small but receptive core of interest in dance which was very different from classical ballet.

In passing we should note that one reason 'modern dance' never gained a very large following in this country was that the British public, until the emergence of the London Contemporary Dance Theatre, was almost totally committed to classical ballet. Unlike Germany and America, where the moderns flourished, Britain had always been noted for a love of ballet, a love which welcomed the stars of the Romantic era, cherished the dancers who graced the great music halls (the Alhambra and the Empire theatres in particular) at the turn of the century – the visiting Russians, adorable Adeline Genée – and from 1911 until 1929 gave Diaghilev what was perhaps his most loyal and discriminating audience.

Yet Isadora Duncan danced in London as early as 1900, making her debut at the Lyceum during the Benson Shakespeare season and following this with a special matinee at St George's Hall under the title *A Happier Age of Gold*. She was greatly admired in London (more so than in America) but did not make quite the impact she did in Paris and on the Continent. Nevertheless, in a chapter entitled 'The Revival of Classical Dancing'*, J. E. Crawford Flitch in his perceptive book *Modern Dancing and Dancers*, published in 1912, described Isadora

---

*Flitch used the word 'classical' to denote dancing which claimed kinship with Greek art; when speaking of ballet he used the word 'academic'.

as 'perhaps the greatest personality who has ever devoted herself to developing the art of dance'. Flitch also noted the popular success of Maud Allan but (rightly) dismissed the sisters Wiesenthal as mere 'pretty fluttering'.

More lasting contributions to a freer style of dance, unrelated to the classic ballet, were made in Britain by Margaret Morris (1891–1980) and Ruby Ginner (1886–1978). Margaret Morris, who had studied with Raymond Duncan, opened a London school in 1910 and by 1912 was appearing with her child dancers at the Court Theatre. She gradually evolved her own method of dancing and in 1925 founded her Margaret Morris Movement which survives today. She had her own small theatre and club in Chelsea during World War I which became a meeting place for dancers, musicians and painters. She also established schools in Manchester, Edinburgh, Glasgow, Aberdeen, Paris and Cannes but in 1939 moved to Glasgow with her painter husband, J. D. Fergusson, and concentrated all her work there. She gradually became more and more interested in the beneficial aspects of dance and movement in relation to health, combining medical and aesthetic values.

Ruby Ginner, like Isadora, drew her inspiration from the dances and the arts of ancient Greece. She formed her own troupe, The Grecian Dancers, in 1913, started her school during World War I and worked with Sybil Thorndike and Lewis Casson on their productions of *The Trojan Women* and other Greek tragedies. She evolved a technique of rhythmic, barefoot dance with a range from lyricism to gymnopaedic, Bacchic and powerful Pyrrhic dance which she named 'The Revived Greek Dance'. In 1923 the Association of Teachers of the Revived Greek Dance was formed (now the Greek Dance Association) and the Ruby Ginner method is still taught throughout the British Isles and by some teachers overseas. It is particularly beneficial for young children and is now even in the curriculum of the Royal Ballet School. In her heyday Ruby Ginner staged vast pageants and in 1930 took a company to Athens to perform in the Delphic Festival. But she thought of her Greek dance as an education in beauty rather than a theatrical spectacle. In his Foreword to her admirable book *Gateway to the Dance*, Professor A. P. Cawadias could write: 'Her theories are founded on the true balance of the physical and psychical parts of man, and upon those words to which the Greeks were addicted – *Adios* and *Sophrosyne*, reverence and restraint.'

We must mention also the work of Madge Atkinson, a beautiful woman and expressive dancer, who evolved a system she called Natural Movement. It may not have been so widely taught as the Margaret Morris or Ruby Ginner styles but it is still greatly admired and lovingly preserved by Miss Atkinson's successors and their pupils.

Crawford Flitch also wrote with enthusiasm of the dancing of Ruth St Denis when she first appeared in London in 1908, ranking her as 'one of the most cultured dancers of the time, and, in her special sphere, certainly the most learned . . . by interpreting the art of the East she has perceptibly broadened the scope of dancing in the west.' Another admirer of Miss Ruth was the ballet critic and historian Cyril W. Beaumont. In an article entitled 'The Art of Ruth St Denis', which appeared in the *Dancing World* in July 1922, he wrote: 'Without any doubt, Miss St Denis is a great artist who may be termed justly a classical dancer.'

Beaumont, however, was primarily interested in and in love with ballet, above all with the Diaghilev Ballet, by whose standards he measured all other undertakings. His attitude towards the Central European school of modern dance is summed up in the severity of his judgement of Mary Wigman. Writing in the *Dance Journal* in June 1932 he proclaimed: 'But, however intellectual her work may be in conception, in realisation – which, after all, is the one thing that matters – it suggests athletics, relieved with phases of dramatic movement, rather than dancing and it is understood in the general conception of the word, and, as such, her work is far more suited to the lecture hall than to the theatre.'

It is no accident that the most influential writers on dancing in the 1920s and 1930s in Britain were balletomanes. Beaumont, the scholar, and Arnold Haskell, the enthusiast, both subscribed to the Diaghilev ideal. Haskell had enormous influence upon public taste in the 1930s. After the runaway success of his book *Balletomania* in 1934 he produced volume after volume extolling first the Ballet Russe companies, then the infant British ballet of which he was an early champion. He could dismiss almost the whole of modern dance in an article he called 'Modern or Merely Gloomy?'.

The situation was very different from that which obtained at the same time in America, where John Martin was so vigorously campaigning for the moderns and so dismissive (until his conversion) of classical ballet.

The one modern dance company which did enjoy popularity in Britain was the Ballets Jooss. They arrived at the Savoy Theatre in 1933 with *The Green Table* and other works and the following year, after the political philosophy of *The Green Table* made it expedient for Jooss (a colleague of Rudolf von Laban) to leave Germany, he made his headquarters at Dartington Hall in Devon. There he directed the Jooss-Leeder School of the Dance with Sigurd Leeder, a dancer and choreographer in his company, who was to remain in London teaching until 1958 and would number many fine dancers among his pupils – among them Jean Cebron. The Dartington Hall Estate, as Lillian Moore explains in her invaluable *Artists of the Dance*

> is a research center for rural arts and crafts. The dance school is only one of its many activities, but the environment which Dartington provides is admirably conducive to creative work and intensive study. The curriculum of the Jooss school includes the techniques of classic and modern dance forms, Choreutic, or space harmony in dancing, Eukinetic, or dancing expression, the Laban method of writing dance script, and composition . . . It seems evident that the Jooss method of training and composition, founded as it is upon a solid technical basis, is far more capable of perpetuation and expansion than some of the more individualistic forms of the modern dance.

But it was not to happen in Britain. Emerging from wartime internment, Jooss moved his company to Cambridge and continued a pattern of touring but in 1951 he returned to Essen and although in 1953 he brought his re-formed company to Sadler's Wells, it broke up later that year. The influence of Jooss today is felt essentially in Germany.

By 1953, of course, the Sadler's Wells Ballet was firmly established as a national treasure at Covent Garden. There had been exhilarating visits from ballet companies from overseas and the wartime 'ballet boom' had built a larger audience than ever before. But to Joe Public, dancegoing meant going to the ballet.

And then, on 1 March 1954, Martha Graham at last brought her company to London, for a three-week season at the Saville Theatre. She brought a large repertory of ten works and created a new one, *Ardent Song*, for London, but at first press and public proved themselves wholly resistant to Graham. Audiences just managed to outnumber the dancers on stage – and it is the theatrical law that if there are more in the auditorium than on stage the show must go on. But by the last couple of days the message had spread and the theatre was nearly full. Significantly, among the afficionados who attended every programme were such artists and figures in the theatre as John Cranko, John Gielgud, Peter Brook, Henry Moore (who became a friend of Graham's at this time), the critic Richard Buckle and a London restaurateur, Robin Howard, who was among the people to be most crucially affected by the season.

1954–1963

◆

By education – Eton and Trinity College, Cambridge – Howard might be thought of as a conventional Englishman who then saw war service as a Lieutenant in the Scots Guards between 1943 and 1945, in that year sustaining injuries so serious that he lost his legs. After the war he studied law and was called to the Bar, although he did not practise. But there was more to Howard than this. His family was distinguished in public service: his father, Sir Arthur Howard, had been a Member of Parliament and was Chairman, under the title of Treasurer, of St Thomas's Hospital. His maternal grandfather was Stanley Baldwin; his great-grandfather was the Canadian railway magnate and philanthropist, Lord Strathcona, and through his mother's family he was also related to Rudyard Kipling. Patronage, in the sense of caring for creative artists, was central to his nature, and in the 1950s Robin Howard gave financial support to an art gallery in which painters whose work he admired were regular exhibitors. Though he had enjoyed Scottish dancing as a boy, his affection and admiration for dance crystalised in the post-war years when the Sadler's Wells Ballet was installed at Covent Garden, and when London knew a wide variety of visiting companies, including those of Roland Petit and the Marquis de Cuevas, American Ballet Theatre and the New York City Ballet. By the early 1950s, though, Robin Howard was beginning to find ballet too predictable and too remote from any concern with spiritual and emotional issues. (It is significant that, for a decade after the Hungarian crisis of 1956, Howard worked for the British United Nations Association, running a refugee department which was soon sending long-term volunteers to work in developing areas, especially in connection with U.N. Agencies.)

Howard had voiced his dissatisfaction with ballet to various friends, especially in relation to the repertory of the ballet at Covent Garden, and it was Peggy Harper, lately returned from the USA, who suggested that he might find greater pleasure in the work of Martha Graham, whose company was due to make its London debut in the following month. Howard's immediate reaction was – significantly for an English ballet enthusiast at this time – to ask who Martha Graham was. The British public might know something about Central European dance – Kurt Jooss was then still a well-remembered and admired choreographer in London – but few English dance-lovers had seen anything of American modern dance.

Robin Howard was bowled over by Graham. 'Though I didn't realise it at the time, my life was undoubtedly changed on that night . . . because not only did I change my immediate arrangements for the following nights so that I saw every performance but one . . . but I also got to know Miss Graham and various members of her company. Ultimately much the most important to me was Robert Cohan, whom I admired immensely as a person and an artist at that time. Many years later, when I was doing something that I never expected to do then – starting a dance organisation – Bob Cohan was my choice for artistic director.'

The impact of the opening Graham performance, as Howard recalls it, was 'shock, and then marvel and wonder. After the first piece, I knew that this was something very important.' And on subsequent evenings what Howard found, for the first time in dancing, was something which 'genuinely spoke to every part of you on many levels. By that I mean particularly spoke to the mind as well as to the heart, and the body, and the spirit . . . Every piece appealed to my intellect, and had an intellectual content. Above all, it had a wholeness.'

Robin Howard's enthusiastic conversion to the Graham ethos was in marked contrast to the reaction of the London audience and the majority of the London dance critics. 'Legend has it' observed Robin Howard, 'that there were only thirty-five people in the stalls on the second night, and I am one of the five thousand people who claim to have been among those thirty-five. I was in fact there.'

In his biography of Graham, Don McDonagh cites one critic who inquired of the Graham visit 'Was this trip necessary?' It was Richard Buckle in the *Observer* who, after initial uncertainty, gave unstinting and perceptive praise during the season and did much to stimulate audiences so that, by the last couple of performances the theatre was full. It was noticeable that many theatre directors and producers, as well as painters, had responded to Buckle's call and had been converted to this novel form of dance.

Howard's one positive action during this 1954 season was to entertain Martha Graham and her company. Since neither the American Embassy nor anyone else seemed prepared to honour Graham's presence in London with a reception, Howard invited the Graham troupe to a dinner at the Gore Hotel, which he owned. He had set up an Elizabethan dining-room there, and so it was that Martha Graham and her dancers met a small group of British admirers and dined on a traditional Elizabethan repast, with Graham herself installed in the Queen's chair at the head of the table.

For the next decade Robin Howard was concerned with many things, largely with his work for the refugee organisation of the United Nations Association, and with several successful enterprises in the hotel and restaurant business.

Then in 1962 Martha Graham undertook an extensive European tour. Although several English papers sent their critics to see the Graham performances, there were no plans for her to visit Britain. Howard learned of this and on asking the reason was told that no impresario was prepared to lose money on a second visit. He was determined that Graham should be seen again in

London. His first contact was with Francis Mason, who was Cultural Affairs Officer at the American Embassy in London and a passionate advocate of all forms of dance. (During his years of service in London, Francis Mason was of inestimable help in promoting interest in American dance, and we here gratefully acknowledge the debt of gratitude that the British public owes to his unstinting service.) Howard remembers Francis Mason suggesting that a fellow enthusiast for Graham was Clive Barnes, then dance critic of the London *Times*. A lunch followed at which it was agreed to invite the Graham company in the following year (1963) with Barnes undertaking to try and prepare the press for the forthcoming season. 'Francis said he would get the Embassy to back it in every way that was possible, and at least to arrange a press conference before they performed, and to give an official party for them. I said I would find someone who knew the business actually to manage them, and I would be the sucker who would lose the money.' Contact was then established with Graham to ensure the season, and Howard set to work. He approached Lord Harewood, then Director of the Edinburgh Festival, who agreed to invite Graham and her company to appear. (Lord Harewood, though most celebrated for his dedication to opera, nevertheless had the good sense to take expert advice concerning the dance offerings at the Festival. It was no accident that he was a friend of Richard Buckle, and his excellent *Opera* magazine had originally run in tandem with Buckle's profoundly influential *Ballet* magazine.)

Robin Howard set about working on the financial aspect of the proposed visit and was advised that he might lose between £10,000 and £20,000.

This, I must say, was a bit of a shock because I wasn't expecting that much. Next time I talked to George Harewood I said 'I want to bring this about, and I am told there may be a loss of this amount. I'm quite prepared to stand the first £10,000 on my own, but the second £10,000 would be difficult. Will you go halves with me if it fails and we need the second £10,000?' So we agreed that between £10,000 and £20,000 he would lose half and I would lose half, if necessary. I've always thought that this was really a very remarkable gesture from him, because I was doing it because I loved the company and was determined that London would pay back the debt it owed them by giving them a really successful next visit. But for George Harewood, who wasn't particularly interested in dance and wasn't committed, to risk his own money in that way was very remarkable.

Graham's season at the Edinburgh Festival did not, in fact, presage a triumph. Dance has rarely been an outright success at the Edinburgh Festival (only the traditional classics of ballet, *Swan Lake* and *The Sleeping Beauty*, seem to attract the ladies from Morningside) and Graham's appearance, at the hideous old Empire Theatre, though it engendered rave notices and what Richard Buckle identified as 'shock, usually followed by a glow of delight and admiration', did not augur well for London. However, so great was the critical acclaim there that her appearances at the Prince of Wales Theatre must be accounted an astonishing triumph, with sold-out houses, ecstatic reception and – all things considered – the most honourable of *amendes* for the lack of interest shown nine years before.

After the 1963 Graham season, Marie Rambert and Patricia Hutchinson saw Robin Howard, and Rambert, with characteristic bluntness, said 'Mr Howard, I don't know who you are or why you've done this, but don't stop now.' Rambert also voiced the opinion that Graham training should be made available to British dancers, and it was this encouragement rather than any deliberate plan on his part – because he had none – which emboldened Robin Howard to approach Martha Graham with the idea of providing training in her school for British dancers, whose expenses Howard would pay.

Robin Howard is very frank about his indebtedness to Marie Rambert. He had not met her prior to Graham's second London season, though he acknowledges that he had always greatly admired the adventurousness of her work. When, after the success of the Graham season, Rambert told Howard 'you mustn't stop now', Howard observes that he 'really paid attention'. Had he not been an admirer of her work and of her personality he might not have proceeded any further. He was an amateur and seized with an amateur's doubts about whether he should continue with something about which he knew so little. He decided quite simply to ask Rambert what he should do and undertake to try and do it. 'I admired her so much and I trusted her, so I tried to do what she said, and it is only because Mim Rambert was so insistent that I did it.' Other people, such as Patricia Hutchinson Mackenzie, gave very sound advice; Ninette de Valois was helpful, 'but she wasn't a *pusher* like Mim, who shoved me into this. Martha advised me against it, saying "If you really want to do it, I will help you but I do advise you not to, because very soon you will find you have no money, no-one will like you, and you'll wish you hadn't done it".'

So a plan was initiated to send selected British dancers for periods of study at the Graham studio, their fees paid for by Robin Howard. The first dancer, Eileen Cropley, arrived in New York at Christmas time, 1963, and the two others chosen at the same time were Anna Price and Christian Holder. They were followed by Timothy Hext and Ross Parks, and three more dancers, who had already made their own way to New York, were given support. These were Clover Roope, Anna Mittelholzer and Irene Dilkes, who were later to dance and teach with the company.

1964-1965

◆

In 1964 the quatercentenary of Shakespeare's birth was marked by an important exhibition at Stratford-upon-Avon organised by Richard Buckle. Robin Howard, who had no connection with this enterprise, had long been fascinated by Shakespeare and had formed a collection of books dealing with the playwright and with his life in Elizabethan England. Since the Shakespeare exhibition would not be seen in London, Howard decided to present a celebration on a rather smaller scale at his Gore Hotel, where the Elizabethan dining-room had introduced a new public to the idea of Elizabethan cuisine. On the first floor of the hotel, decorated to suggest what the backstage of the Globe Theatre might have been like, Howard assembled a fascinating collection of largely bibliographic materials for display, whose core was his own collection. This included the first four Shakespeare folios, a quarto, the first published edition of Shakespeare's poems and a very considerable collection of Elizabethan and Jacobean plays, as well as books on husbandry and collections of recipes. (This was all later to be sold at auction to help secure the work of the Contemporary Dance Trust.) To assist him in the organisation of this exhibition Howard engaged a new secretary. She was Janet Eager, who was to become equally involved with the Contemporary Dance Trust and has remained with it, as its administrator, ever since.

On 25 November 1964 a document was prepared, duplicated and sent out to interested persons under the title 'Formation of Trust for Modern Dance'. The document noted that this 'Robin Howard Trust' was originated 'after many requests were received during and immediately following the Martha Graham season'. Its declared object was to help people in Britain keep more in touch with dance developments abroad and to experiment more, and the proposed method was to encourage greater interest in American dance. This was to be done under the following headings:

(a) Bringing American companies here, or co-operating with others who are doing so. (b) Bringing American teachers here – two top members of the Graham company have promised to come over for a minimum of two months between April and June 1965. Ballet Rambert, the Rambert School, Western Theatre Ballet, London Dance Theatre and the Arts Educational Trust have already asked to use these teachers and other organisations will be approached. Classes for individual dancers are guaranteed. (c) Martha Graham has promised to give free tuition to up to ten students per year in her school for the next few years. A basic selection committee has already been formed – Dame Marie Rambert, Miss Christyne Lawson (the only former member of the Graham company permanently resident in this country), Mr Francis Mason, Assistant Cultural Attaché at the United States Embassy, and Mr Robin Howard. Other British dancers and teachers have promised to help with auditions.

The Trust document continued by noting that it had given token grants to Rambert and Western Theatre Ballet, and that funds had enabled London Dance Theatre to give a London season, and there were also discussions to try and enable other small companies to appear in the metropolis. With regard to finance it was noted that a trust was being formed to carry on funding, and an initial £20,000 had been promised. The document also observed that the fund would be increased to £25,000 'if the current Paul Taylor season does not lose too much'! It was hoped that £50,000 might be raised within six months and that, with sufficient support, a permanent studio would be set up, open to established teachers of modern dance. 'Later still a small touring contemporary dance company may be helped to start but only if there is a need for it and there is room for it. It is also intended that eventually to arrange (sic) exchanges with countries other than the United States.'

The news of the setting up of this trust was timed to coincide with the Paul Taylor season at the Princes (now Shaftesbury) Theatre in order to stimulate public interest, and it was announced that Taylor had offered full co-operation for the future if anyone wished to mount any of his works, either a revival or a creation. Merce Cunningham and Alvin Ailey had also been consulted and had agreed to help.

On 2 April 1965 the Trust Deed was signed, setting up the first Trust to cope with the initial tasks of educating public and dancers alike in the ideas of the Graham technique. The Deed stated that Robin Howard, 'being desirous of establishing a charitable trust to foster promote and increase the interest of the public in the knowledge understanding and practice of the art of the ballet and to promote and assist presentations of the ballet and the training of ballet dancers and choreographers', had set aside certain sums. The document further declared that 'the ballet and ballet dancing shall mean modern ballet and modern ballet dancing in all its forms and expressions'. It is intriguing to note that initially the term 'ballet' had to be used.*

Within three days the trustees had had a first meeting, and on 10 April a second meeting announced that Dame Marie Rambert, Mrs Bridget Campbell, Miss

*The reason for this was that Robin Howard had been given legal advice that 'ballet would be considered artistic and educational, therefore charitable, but the word "dance" was suspect and legally might and probably would be assumed to mean something non-cultural and non-charitable. We had to use the term "modern ballet" to mean "modern dance". Only once we had been in existence for three years, and had shown what we were doing was genuinely charitable, did we dare change the name.'

Ann Hutchinson, Miss Pat Hutchinson, Miss Brigitte Kelly and Miss Christyne Lawson had agreed to serve as a temporary advisory committee. A plan was announced for the next three months, starting on 26 April 1965, to bring over three Graham dancer/teachers from New York and to use them and two Graham-trained teachers already in the country (Eileen Cropley and Christyne Lawson) to audition students and give demonstrations. This included a week of performances with the Royal Ballet under the auspices of the newly-formed Ballet for All. The minimum age for students was sixteen and each was initially to be given a series of twelve introductory classes, 'so as to spread the opportunity but to give more classes to some of the best'.

Six weeks later the Trust announced its implementation of the first phase of its work. Ethel Winter and Robert Powell, two of the finest dancers in the Graham company, had agreed to give classes in London between May and July 1965 – though in the event Winter was joined by Mary Hinkson and, later, Bertram Ross. 'There will be separate beginners and intermediate classes, for ballet dancers, for modern and jazz dancers and for "others". A charge of 7s 6d per student per class will be made, and students will be expected to participate in three classes a week for the minimum period of one month.' Further, Ethel Winter and her colleagues were announced as giving classes to ballet companies and dance schools, and auditions were to be held in June and July to select students who would spend a year at the Graham school in New York.

Ironically, this scheme for study in New York was to run into difficulties after a year when it proved to be too successful. The students were finding jobs in America and were opting to stay in order to dance with major companies, rather than returning to the non-existent employment possibilities in Britain.

Advertisements were placed in the *Dancing Times* and *Dance and Dancers* with the idea of recruiting a group of students who would follow a single course of instruction. In the event there were so many applicants (Janet Eager recalls more than 200 aspirants) that in place of the intended long-term course there had to be more courses for more people, but shorter in span. The Trust had no premises, and thus it was that each night Janet Eager travelled round London in a van with rolls of linoleum which she put down each night in a different place. On Monday night a home had been found at the Arts Educational Trust, then at Hyde Park Corner. On Tuesday night, classes were held at the Mercury Theatre, Notting Hill Gate (birthplace of the Ballet Rambert). On Wednesday afternoon the Africa Centre in King Street, Covent Garden, was pressed into service. Thursday night found the students back at Arts Educational. On Friday the Mercury was hired again and on Saturday morning the setting was Victor Silvester's ballroom in the Odeon Cinema, King's Road, Chelsea.

Classes were scheduled for beginners, elementary and intermediate level and from the start numbers were sufficient to justify two classes in each group. The success of the first classes given by Mary Hinkson, Ethel Winter and Bertram Ross led to an immediate decision to spread the gospel through the use of a very small demonstration group which performed in university towns, such as Oxford, and a few other large cities such as Eastbourne. These even pre-dated the important demonstrations master-minded by Peter Brinson and his Ballet for All group which had started a year before. (This was a demonstration group, developed from an idea of Peter Brinson, which presented 'ballet plays', combining narration and dance in a theatrical context with costumes, props, minimal scenery and piano accompaniment, to focus on a single theme and introduce a particular ballet or a particular period in ballet history to audiences in small theatres, or in schools and colleges.)

A third and final meeting of the Robin Howard Trust with the advisory committee on 23 August 1965 summed up the achievement of the past three months. It noted that Martha Graham had talked to the students and visited the Rambert School and the Arts Educational Trust during a short visit to London. Bertram Ross had visited for two-and-a-half weeks in early July, and the work of Mary Hinkson, who was in artistic control of the programme for the first period, and of Ethel Winter for the last period, was commended. Christyne Lawson and Eileen Cropley had joined the main Graham company members as performers, demonstrators and occasional teachers. Miss Judyth Knight had played the piano for all the demonstrations and for most of the classes (and has remained ever since as a pianist with the Trust). Altogether 137 classes had been held, attended by over 200 students, who represented 70% of the people who had auditioned.

Demonstrations had been held for the Royal Ballet School, the Rambert School, Bush Davies, the Imperial Society of Teachers of Dancing, and the London Central Stage Group, for the London Ballet Circle and the Oxford Ballet Club, for a special study group at Dartington College and at Nonington College of Physical Education. A special demonstration was also given at the LAMDA theatre for interested people. Furthermore, the Trust had joined with the Royal Opera House in presenting a one-week season of Ballet for All at the Theatre Royal, Stratford East, where, for the first time, dancers of the Royal Ballet and the Martha Graham company appeared on stage together. As a bonus, funds had also been made available to enable the Trust's students to purchase tickets at specially reduced prices for the Bolshoi Ballet, which had been appearing at Covent Garden that summer. In summing up the achievements of the past three months the Trust was able to observe that 'the response to the classes and demonstrations was far greater than had been envisaged ... both because of the exceptionally high standard of the Graham representatives and because countless people saw in the disciplined professional Graham approach to contemporary dance for the theatre something which is lacking and needed in Britain.'

After acknowledging thanks to various schools who had supported this first essay, not least by making studios available, Robin Howard noted that 'The Trust would do a great service to the dance in Britain if it could get a school of contemporary dance established. This in my submission is an immediate need. It will however require more money than the Trust alone can provide. The next need is for help for would-be choreographers.' The advisory committee headed by Dame Marie Rambert was then disbanded, but not before the trustees had discussed future policy and agreed to support the idea of the proposed new school. In the interim, classes were to continue from 2 September and Robin Howard was authorised to spend up to £1,500 on these classes until December. 'They instructed the director to start immediately trying to prepare for the new school by seeking patrons, other financial support and premises. They indicated that they would try to make £5,000 available for the capital needs of the school, and £1,000 a year for its running expenses for the first five years.'

As we have said, the performances at the Theatre Royal, Stratford East, during the first week of July 1965, came under the umbrella of Ballet for All. The Stratford performances were billed as Ballet for All but, as the *Financial Times* review commented on 8 July:

> ... a better title for this programme would be Martha Graham for All, since this one week season offers the fascinating sight of two vital elements in the twentieth century dancing in direct confrontation. The first part of the programme each night provides the analysis of some fragment of classical dancing (when I saw the performance last night the first Odette/Siegfried duet from *Swan Lake* was studied); the second part is devoted to an introduction to the Martha Graham school followed by a series of extracts from her works ... The special cachet of course lies in the presence of three of Graham's dancers – Mary Hinkson, Ethel Winter and Bertram Ross, together with two other Graham-trained artists, Christyne Lawson and Eileen Cropley. Their half of the proceedings offers a preparatory class, with its floor work and falls, and then six dances that place the schooling within the context of the theatre ... we can renew acquaintance with *Diversion of Angels*, *Embattled Garden*, *Clytemnestra*, and *Seraphic Dialogue* and there is a fragment from *Samson Agonistes*, not yet seen here, showing Delilah seducing and betraying Samson, which has tremendous erotic imagery. It goes without saying that the dancers are as magnificent as ever; Ross is a tower of strength, and the artistry of the women burns bright even in the regrettably brief fragments ... The final curtain calls provide a sight that must surely be unique – and let us hope significant – for London balletgoers, as Bertram Ross leads on Miss Landon [Jane Landon of the Royal Ballet, who had danced Odette in the programme] to take a call: amazingly different they may be in training and aesthetic aims, but they are, after all, both dancers.

1966–1968

◆

In March 1966 the Robin Howard Trust invited critics and well-wishers to a demonstration to be held at Queen Alexandra's House in Kensington Gore, London, on 30 April and 2 May, in which the students sponsored by the Trust 'will show class work and simple combinations, then Miss Patricia Christopher and our resident teachers will continue with more advanced work.' Patricia Christopher, a Graham graduate, taught at the Graham school in New York and had danced with José Limón, Pearl Lang and Yuriko. The resident teachers were Eileen Cropley, who had been a pupil of Sigurd Leeder before becoming one of the first students sent by the Trust to work at the Graham school, and was now scheduled to join the Paul Taylor company; Anna Mittelholzer, another advanced student at the Graham school; Clover Roope, formerly with the Royal Ballet and subsequently with Western Theatre Ballet, who had won a Harkness Fellowship to study dance in America; and Timothy Hext, who had also studied with Graham. The second purpose of the demonstration was:

> to give you a further, and possibly last, report from the Robin Howard Trust since we hope, at the demonstrations, to be able to announce the formation of a new and larger trust and a permanent school of contemporary dance . . . Since our last report we have continued to support the contemporary dance classes in London. About thirty students have attended these regularly and another fifteen whenever they can (most are also students of classical ballet and aged between 16 and 23). In addition a new class of 20 beginners started on March 7, and on May 3 regular special mid-day classes will start for professional dancers. Of the regular students ten have so far reached the inter-mediate stage.

It was with evident pride that the report noted that five other students from Britain were working at the Graham school and were either supported by the Trust or had won places as a result of the London auditions. The two largest additional disbursements had been £2,500 in 1964 and 1966, which had enabled London Dance Theatre, directed by Jack Carter and Norman McDowell, to hold seasons of classical ballet at the Lyric Theatre, Hammersmith and the Vaudeville Theatre in the Strand, and a grant of £500 in 1966 to help Ballet Rambert present a new work, with a promise of a further £500. Aid to Rambert 'had only been limited by resources'.

The report ended by observing that 'the trustees have had to use up some of their own capital and to borrow further money to pay out sums far greater than their income. This they have gladly done, but it must now be for the new Trust . . . to continue and extend the work which has begun and which has been welcomed so enthusiastically.'

In 1966 the Robin Howard Trust was replaced by a new organisation, Contemporary Ballet Trust Ltd, which was officially constituted in July of that year. Preliminary discussions took place in the spring when a group of trustees was first invited to discuss the aims and policies of the new organisation. At its first meeting on 2 March 1966 at his Gore restaurant in Queen's Gate, Robin Howard explained that the object of the meeting was to discuss the feasibility of setting up a new Trust to support contemporary dance and especially to continue and expand the work already started by the Robin Howard Trust. It was proposed that a trust company with a council of management would initially aim to take over and administer the school and run an appeal for funds. The school was to have six patrons, and the Earl of Harewood, Sir John Gielgud, Henry Moore, Ninette de Valois and Marie Rambert joined Martha Graham in agreeing to serve. Furthermore, the five British patrons would also serve as patrons of the appeal. The first object, declared the minutes of the meeting, would be to start and support a school of contemporary dance in London. Robin Howard then explained why the word 'ballet' had to be retained in the Trust's official title, but went on to state that the school would be called the London College of Contemporary Dance. A proviso was also included in the draft articles of the Trust which would give the Trust's solicitor, G. C. W. Radcliffe, power to set up schools wherever the Trust might require them: this would also be relevant 'so that we could set up a dance company or companies if this was desirable later'. The appeal was to seek to raise £17,000 by the end of the year and 'not to try for a large capital sum until 1967 or later'.

The Articles of Association of the Contemporary Ballet Trust Limited, which was incorporated on 8 July 1966 as a limited company but without share capital, reiterated the intention to foster, promote and increase public interest in contemporary dance and envisaged every sort of activity connected with this aim. It served as an umbrella for all the future manifestations of Robin Howard's plans for contemporary dance in Britain.

The inception of the Trust seems to have marked a decisive moment in the history of the Howard enterprise. The year 1966 had already brought demonstrations by Betty de Jong of the Taylor company with pupils of the Trust's classes in front of an invited audience, and a performance at the American Embassy led by the Graham dancer Yuriko, when she visited London. There followed further lecture demonstrations both for the press and for audiences arranged by Patricia Christopher, who was resident teacher, with dancers including Anna Mittelholzer, Anna Price, Clover Roope, Timothy Hext and Jack Nightingale. Eight British dancers were awarded scholarships to study in New York at the Graham school. In May, having led for the past year an itinerant existence which

had involved work in no fewer than seventeen different studios, the School at last found a permanent location in 5–7 Berners Place. Here, in what had been an old clothing showroom just north of Oxford Circus, the School could find a resting place, somewhat limited in space but at least its own.

When these premises were found, Janet Eager became officially the administrator as well as acting as general factotum to the Trust. The premises consisted of one large studio and two changing rooms – 'which we shared with the mice', she recalls – and a bathroom-cum-lavatory shared with the furrier whose premises were above. By knocking down partitions they were able to produce a dance studio 60 feet by 30 feet. Neighbouring offices complained of the noise of the dancers and the music; the roof leaked, and though there were buckets placed on the piano to catch the water, there were no showers or any other amenities for the students.

In September of that year the London School of Contemporary Dance began its first term. Students were offered the choice of enrolling for a full academic year or attending individual classes. Inevitably the main technique taught was that of Martha Graham, but classical ballet training was also offered and from the very first there were classes in composition and choreography. Martha Graham became closely involved with the School, not only as its artistic adviser but also because she furnished three important teachers when, as guests from her company, Takako Asakawa, Robert Powell and Dudley Williams came to London to work at the School. Graham's involvement underlined the fact that the London School of Contemporary Dance was the only institution other than the Graham School itself authorised to teach Graham technique. This was necessary in order to refute the aims of numerous practitioners who, having attended a few Graham classes, were proposing to offer instruction in Graham technique on the slenderest of qualifications.

During the first year at Berners Place the organisation felt very much like a studio rather than a school until the arrival of Pat Hutchinson (Mackenzie) as director of the school in September 1967. Miss Hutchinson organised a schedule of classes from 9 am to 6 pm, with additional evening sessions. Even though the school was essentially funded by Robin Howard, the students were asked to contribute something to the cost of their classes and Howard provided scholarships for certain deserving aspirants.

The intellectual needs of the students were taken care of too, initially by Robin Howard's donation of his own collection of dance books, a collection which has been expanded over the years to the admirable library and archive of today. Patrick Steede, a graduate from Dartington, joined the faculty to oversee the students in visits to galleries and the theatre, while the critic Fernau Hall lectured on the history of dance.

Among the students who joined at this time were Robert North and Linda Gibbs – North as a Royal Ballet School student who was granted permission to come and study contemporary dance; Gibbs as a Rambert dancer who had

Robert Powell in Robert Cohan's Sky *(1967)*

left the company at the time of its crucial change of identity in 1966 when Norman Morrice engineered its new policy as a modern dance group. Two other students from this time were also to make names for themselves; Richard Alston and Siobhan (Sue) Davies. Siobhan Davies was an art student attracted to the idea of dance; Alston too had art school training, but it was only his persistence in returning to ask to join classes that eventually won him a place in the School.

As Robin Howard recalls of these early days:

> Since there were no grants for our students, we offered twelve of them free tuition in return for doing odd jobs about the building. Jack Nightingale, for instance, who subsequently danced with us and then with Paul Taylor, and Namron . . . [subsequently a member of the London Contemporary Dance Theatre for many years] were responsible for sweeping out the premises and doing any heavy carrying . . . I still expected some choreographic genius to appear and provide work for our students. Partly to encourage the appearance of this genius, partly because I believed that actual performance was so vital to the development of the dance student, but most of all just because some of our first budding choreographers were ready for this experience, we arranged for their first works to be shown that same autumn in programmes presented by Balletmakers. Incidentally, I have never felt that Balletmakers and Teresa Early, its guiding hand, have ever been given sufficient recognition for the highly important work they did at this time.

*

In 1966 Robert Cohan was an associate director of the Martha Graham company. After the 1963 Graham season in London he had torn his Achilles tendon, but with careful work he had recovered all his former power as a dancer and was performing leading roles with Graham as well as choreographing and dancing with his own group between Graham's seasons. Early in 1966 Cohan renewed acquaintance with Robin Howard, when he came to New York to work as administrative director of the Graham School and company. Howard was now also deeply involved with the possible further development of his Trust in London and it was evident that he needed to rely upon a major figure in the Graham organisation for advice and guidance. Essentially he was looking for someone to come to London to head a school which would develop into a company, and on Graham's advice he decided to approach Cohan. For Cohan such a change would be traumatic, since he was a New Yorker born and bred, and indeed his first decision was to try and have the best of both worlds by commuting between London and New York. He agreed to come to London in the spring of 1967, at the end of the Graham company's tour to Portugal, with the intention of devising a programme that could be performed in the summer of that year. Starting work in London, however, he soon realised that the dancers were as yet unable to speak the Graham language with any security. Thus he made the

decision to teach them certain dances as it were by rote rather than present a performance of fully-comprehended Graham technique.

It was also decided to give a performance outside London, at the new Adeline Genée Theatre, East Grinstead, in October. The intention was to display some of the creative work which was already an important aspect of the School's identity, and choreographies by Anna Mittelholzer, Jacqui Lyons and Patrick Steede, as well as works specially made by Cohan, were featured on the programme. These were rehearsed to concert pitch and, to provide the very necessary Graham presence for the occasion, two eminent Graham dancers, Robert Powell and Noemi Lapzeson, were invited to join Cohan as dancers in the programme.

The first performance of the Contemporary Dance Group in October 1967

Robert Cohan rehearsing Noemi Lapzeson and Robert Powell in Sky

– aided by a £2,000 grant from the Arts Council – was in effect the real beginning of the company. For the five-day season between Tuesday 10 October and Saturday 14 October, a programme entitled *Dance, One, Two. Four* was presented by the Contemporary Ballet Trust Limited. The programme contained a note from Robin Howard explaining the title:

> *Dance One, Two. Four* is presented by the Contemporary Ballet Trust one year after the Trust founded the London School of Contemporary Dance, two years after most of the performers started Graham classes, and four years after the first sponsored British dancers were sent to the Martha Graham School in New York. Our artistic director, Robert Cohan (after much hesitation) accepted a difficult brief: to put as many students as possible on stage in a way which would tax but not over-extend them, to show recent workshop ballets, to create parts for some of our most promising dancers and to put all this into a programme with works of his own for established members of the Martha Graham company.
>
> The Adeline Genée Theatre has been chosen for the first performances because of its very good stage and its small auditorium. If all goes according to plan our dancers will gain extra experience over the winter and be joined by others now in America – and we shall get some new works. Then we hope to perform in London, and eventually to form a permanent, professional Contemporary Dance Company. One week after this week's performances, four dancers start a 'Ballet for All' type of tour to show contemporary dance to schools and small theatres anywhere in Britain. For such a new enterprise, bookings are encouraging but we still have several dates free, especially from about 10 November to 10 December.

Robin Howard's comment takes us to the heart of the achievements and aspirations of this season. From the Graham company came not only Robert Cohan but also Robert Powell and Noemi Lapzeson, who led a company of eighteen named dancers supported by 'students of the London School of Contemporary Dance'. Among the listed dancers were Robert Dodson (now Robert North) and David Earle, the Canadian dancer-choreographer then teaching at the London School of Contemporary Dance, and the entire production was directed by Robert Cohan. The gala evening preview of the Contemporary Dance Group on 10 October began with the world premiere of Cohan's *Tzaikerk* (Evening Song) for six women from the company, followed by *Piece for Metronome and Three Dancers* which had originally been choreographed by Patrick Steede at Dartington College in the spring of 1967 and was included in the programme as an example of a different tradition of contemporary dance. After the interval came *Family of Man* by Anna Mittelholzer, the first example of choreography springing from the traditions of the Contemporary Dance School itself, and the evening ended with two more works by Cohan, the British premiere of his duet *Eclipse*, danced by Noemi Lapzeson and Robert Powell, and the first performance of *Sky*, which was to stay in the repertory for many years. Later in the week Cohan also introduced the British premiere of his *Hunter of Angels*, in which he danced Jacob in the Biblical story of Jacob and the Angel (this role taken by Robert Powell), and there was also the British premiere of *Witness of Innocence*, a dance work about Lady Jane Grey by David Earle. The acknowledgements for this dance drama noted that the production was 'staged thanks to a grant from the Elizabethan Rooms which present Tudor food and entertainment every night in Queensgate (sic), London'. The generous hand of Robin Howard was evident even here.

Robin Howard had already acknowledged the support given to him by the press, and now the major London newspapers were generous in their comment upon this very first enterprise, with extensive coverage in *The Times*, the *Guardian*, the *Financial Times*, the *Daily Telegraph*, and the *Observer* as well as the *Scotsman*. Alexander Bland in the *Observer* was typical in his response to the season: 'Though its indefatigable inspirer and guardian angel, Robin Howard, cautiously announced that the programme ... was only a preamble to the company's permanent establishment, it is clear that in effect the deed is done and that last Tuesday will be celebrated as the fateful birthday. It is fair, then, to record that the Contemporary Dance Group has got away to an excellent start.'

Following this launching of the company, several of the objectives announced by Robin Howard in his programme note were achieved. The School initiated courses lasting both one and three years under the directorship of Patricia Hutchinson, and a group of dancers set out on a tour of arts centres and colleges spreading the gospel of contemporary dance.

The year 1968 represented for the Trust, its School and its demonstration group a period of expansion and of consolidation. In the prime area of discovering choreographic talent and encouraging creativity, the Group and the students gave two workshop performances at the LAMDA (London Academy of Music and Dramatic Art) Theatre in West Kensington on 12 and 13 January, and then two more on 18 and 19 February. At these performances sixteen new works were presented, of which nine were the creation of debutant choreographers. Furthermore, the Dance Group travelled extensively performing throughout the country at colleges, occasionally in theatres and schools. It gave a programme whose first part was a lecture demonstration, in emulation of Ballet for All's work, which explained the Martha Graham technique and followed this with a second part containing 'new contemporary dance works by British and American choreographers'.

The company visited locations as diverse as Dartington College near Totnes, Devon, in February; Ravensbourne College of Arts and Design, Maidstone, Kent; and the Liverpool Festival in March. With Arts Council funding the group visited Northern Ireland in late March and early April, and then proceeded to Glasgow University on 20 April and the Stables Theatre, Hastings in May, allow-

ing London a first proper sight of the Group's work at the Collegiate Theatre (now the Bloomsbury) in Gordon Street on 16 May at a gala performance in aid of the Malcolm Sargent Cancer Fund for Children. This was followed two days later by a first public performance of 'new works including some first works by young choreographers'. The London showings brought works by Cohan (*Tzaikerk*) and a fragment by Paul Taylor, 'Hand Dance' from his *Piece Period*. The various other choreographers were: Vivien Gear; Rebecca Wilson (from Canada); Ruth Posner, a London School of Contemporary Dance student; Richard Alston, showing his first work, *Transit*; Barry Moreland, also presenting a first work, *Dark Voyage*; Henrietta Lyons, whose first work was *Interchange*; Alan Beattie; Mavis Crabtree and Anna Mittelholzer.

The programmes were directed by David Earle, a graduate of the National Ballet School of Canada and then of the Martha Graham School. He had danced with José Limón, among others, and he was to be a teacher during the early years of the School. The Group tours went on through June and, after a summer break, continued with extensive touring in October with visits to Leeds, to Repton School, to the Chelsea College of Physical Education in Eastbourne and the Worcester College of Education for the Worcester Festival. The British Isles were being educated.

Talking about the work of the School at this time, Robin Howard noted that, in addition to the main body of Graham technique classes (eight or nine a week), the LSCD students had three classical classes a week and three music sessions concerned both with appreciation and understanding. There were also studies in dance history, anatomy and philosophy. Part-time students were accepted from the age of fourteen and full-time students from the age of sixteen. Discussing the general implications of the work over the past four years Robin Howard could observe 'We have something established now and it is purely a question of money as to how stable it will be . . . We have had about fifty bookings since we established the touring group at the end of last October [1967] and during this time we have had just two months off. The performances of the group owe a lot to those of Ballet for All. We have four dancers, a speaker and a pianist. We go mainly to schools and teacher training colleges and have only been to about three or four commercial theatres.'

During 1967–68 Robert Cohan rehearsed and guided this small group in the lecture demonstrations by which the Trust was spreading contemporary dance round Britain and giving dance experience to its members. But Cohan was also criss-crossing the Atlantic between his London duties and the demands of the Graham seasons in America – teaching in London and performing in New York. Then, as the School continued to develop and there was already talk of the move to new premises called The Place, it was clear that a crisis was approaching. At Christmas 1968 Cohan was back in New York to prepare for a season with Martha Graham. It so happened that there were no rehearsals scheduled and, as he sat one evening in Noemi Lapzeson's house in Brooklyn, Cohan asked

Robert Cohan and Noemi Lapzeson in Martha Graham's El Penitente, *first staged by LCDT in 1969*

himself 'What am I doing here, when they need me so desperately in London?'

A decision had to be taken, and gathering together what immediate cash he could from his own wallet and Noemi Lapzeson's, Cohan called up British Airways and asked for an immediate flight to London. The first plane left next morning. Cohan booked a one-way ticket, dined with Noemi Lapzeson who then drove him to his house where he packed, wrote a note to Graham announcing that he would not be in rehearsal the next day, and flew to London. In London during the next six weeks he made up his mind.

> I realised that when I was away from New York the Graham company got on quite well without me, while the London Contemporary Dance Group started to fall apart if I was away. So Martha Graham's spring season in New York in 1969 was my last one. I had seen The Place. We worked all through the summer of 1969 preparing for our season and I didn't go back to New York for three years. I had made up my mind. I was here in London to stay.

1969

◆

On 16 January 1969 a press release from the Contemporary Ballet Trust announced that the Trust

... would be setting up a new arts centre in London within the next two months.

The new centre, the first of its kind in the world, is to be housed in the former Drill Hall of the Artists' Rifles in Duke's Road, Euston. Mr Howard signed the 21 year lease today. The area, over 15,000 square feet, will contain a small experimental studio/theatre suitable for dance, drama and concert performances, and will seat approximately 300.

There will be five large studies, three smaller rehearsal rooms and a canteen. Ultimately there are plans to build a small restaurant which will seat 150. The building will also serve as the headquarters for the London School of Contemporary Dance and the Contemporary Ballet Trust's administrative offices. Audiences for theatre performances will be limited to members only ... Mr Howard plans that the new centre will be experimental headquarters not only for dancers but also for musicians, painters, sculptors, and all those who are involved in the allied arts. The first associates in the venture are the Pierrot Players, founded by the composers Peter Maxwell Davies and Harrison Birtwistle. Others will be announced later. There will be a permanent classical ballet studio for Madame Cléo Nordi.

It is planned that running costs of the new centre will be paid by renting out the theatre and studio space throughout the year. The Trust plans to use the theatre at regular intervals throughout the year of its own Company, Group and Workshop. The Artistic Director is Mr Robert Cohan.

Mr Howard stressed the need for co-operation between the Arts, saying that dance in particular would die without the stimulation of new musicians, designers, directors and sculptors. It had always been the Trust's policy to create this sort of involvement, as witness the Patrons of the School who included Lord Harewood, Sir John Gielgud and Mr Henry Moore. The move to the new premises is evidence of the extension of this policy, though the move is earlier than expected.

Whilst acknowledging the assistance from the Arts Council, Lord Goodman, Mr John Cruft and Mr David Reynolds in particular, Mr Howard continued by saying he appreciated their difficulties caused by lack of funds and the need of giving priority to existing organisations. 'However,' he said, 'we were bound to go bankrupt or lower our standards if we continued as before. So we decided to take a calculated risk; to do more and not less and to push on even faster with our plans because in this way we believe we have a better chance of getting the money we require. It has involved turning ourselves into business people as well as artistic people. But we could see no alternative and in some ways it may even be a good thing.'

The London School of Contemporary Dance will move to the new premises over the Easter holiday and then it will be possible to give more details of the Trust's associates.

Mr Howard paid tribute to the help from the landlords, the United Kingdom Provident Institution. He felt, he said, that the premises would be rightly used. The headquarters of Artists in War had become the headquarters of Arts in Peace.

It was obvious that the School had to expand and find premises more suited to the needs of its increasing number of students. It was obvious, too, that the touring group must have a home and a chance to develop into the company that Howard and Cohan had intended. The discovery of the disused headquarters of the Artists' Rifles was one of those fortunate finds which might be seen to counterbalance the difficulties which Robin Howard and his group were so manfully surmounting.

It is important to remember, however, that, in Robin Howard's own words, 'We never had more than nine years security at The Place when we signed the lease, but it was subject to the right of the landlords to terminate under certain conditions, one of which was if they wished to develop the site, which of course they did later on. I can remember thinking and saying at the time that it was worth it because, within nine years we would either be bankrupt or have become a success, which other people would not wish to see die.'

Behind the facts as presented by Robin Howard there was, of course, the calculated gamble of making The Place a viable enterprise. Seven months after the signing of the lease a vast amount had already been achieved. B. A. Young, drama critic of the *Financial Times*, wrote in that paper on 19 August of The Place as it now was and as he had known it earlier during his Army career. Speaking of The Place – the name had emerged after a first discussion had suggested calling it The Artist's Place – Young noted that:

. . . behind that bald address lies three quarters of a century of contemporary history, for between 1889 and 1967, No 17 Duke's Road was the headquarters of the Artists' Rifles.

Rationalisation of the Territorial Army to post-war conditions has moved the Artists, in their latest incarnation as 21st Special Air Service Regiment, to the Duke of York's headquarters in Chelsea and there is something artistically satisfying in the occupation of their former home by an organisation like the Contemporary Ballet Trust. It's true that the arts are not much practised in the Regiment* now; but former members have included such names as Lord Leighton, G. F. Watts, Holman Hunt, William Morris, Brandon (*Charley's Aunt*) Thomas, Noël Coward and me. The first headquarters was at Burlington House, the next at the Arts Club. That Duke's Road should be taken over by an artistic enterprise is entirely appropriate.

The Drill Hall, on a stage at the end of which my own brief career as a dancer ran its ephemeral course, is now hardly recognisable. Seating for 400 has been installed on a steep rake leading up to the windows of the Serjeants' Mess, leaving a generous space for a floor level stage at the end (the end where you go down the stairs to the Signals Office). There is room for a big studio under the seating. There's another big studio in the Canteen, and several smaller ones throughout the building. Appropriately A, B and C Company Offices are now Dressing Rooms A, B and C. The miniature range has been divided by partitions into studio, wardrobe and workshop.

If this constant harping back to military origins seems a bit nostalgic, you should see the nostalgia that goes on at The Place as it is now called. There never were such partisans of the Regiment outside its own ranks. There's an old wooden letter-rack in the office of the executive director, Annette Massie (once the office of the C.O. and the Adjutant). 'I don't know what I can use it for,' she said. 'We found it in the basement. I can't *bear* to let it go.' To return to the present, what about the Contemporary Ballet Trust? . . . The organisation includes the Dance Company, formed last year, 10 to 16 strong, with a repertoire of works by major contemporary choreographers; the Dance Group, a nucleus of four dancers and a speaker, with special programmes for schools, colleges and small theatres, a lecture/demonstration or film programme designed to give instant information and entertainment to even smaller audiences; the Workshop where young choreographers, designers, dancers and musicians can see their work tried out; and the School, which under Patricia Hutchinson is now in its third academic year.

During the move and in the succeeding months the Contemporary Dance Group continued its wide-ranging demonstration tours with a programme which began with an explanation of Graham technique, and continued with a group of new contemporary dance works by British and American choreographers.* For the Camden Festival, which ran from 3 May until 1 June, the Dance Group announced two performances at the Collegiate Theatre. The first, on 20 May, was the usual combination of lecture/demonstration introduced by Robert Cohan followed by examples of contemporary choreography. The second, on

*Robin Howard discovered he had a double connection with the Artists' Rifles. His relative, the painter Burne-Jones, was one of the early and very enthusiastic volunteers; his uncle, Lord Strathcona, was the Colonel of the Regiment in 1939.

*One of the first performances was in a basement room in what is now called the Kennedy Centre near Regent's Park, in aid of the Camden Committee for Race Relations.

22 May, was an opportunity to show some of the new works being created under the Group's auspices and three new works were scheduled: Barry Moreland's *Summer Games* to music by Samuel Barber; Clover Roope's *O Saisons, O Châteaux* with a score by Elizabeth Lutyens; and Ruth Posner's *Four Poems* which was danced to the words of e e cummings, Yeats and Keats. The anticipated debut by the company was postponed until September 'owing to alterations to the new premises, Artists' Rifles Drill Hall in Euston, being behind schedule.' London had already had a chance of seeing the work of the Group when, on 10 May, eight of the dancers were seen at the University of London Convocation performing a selection from the repertory. In the summer of this same year the Group made its first foreign tour when it visited France in July, performing the demonstration programme at Vichy (on a stage 22′ × 17′) and following this with performances on 8 and 10 July at Vichy, on 15 July at Chateauvallon, and on 17 July at Les Baux. These performances involved the full company led by Robert Cohan, with Noemi Lapzeson and William Louther (from the Graham company) as guests. The reception in France of a strongly representative repertory – Cohan's *Tziakerk*, *Eclipse* and *Shanta Quintet*, Clover Roope's *Solo* and *Trio for Two*, and Alvin Ailey's *Hermit Songs* for William Louther – was enthusiastic, if at times slightly uncomprehending.

One newspaper thought that Robin Howard was responsible for the choreography; another called one of the ballets *shy*; but there were also references to 'fine artists whose conviction and worth must be stressed'.

At last, on 2 September, came the official opening of The Place by Lord Goodman, Chairman of the Arts Council, and the first performance by the company its own theatre. The season was to run for three weeks with a repertory of twelve works by Cohan, Patricia Christopher, Barry Moreland and Clover Roope, Ailey's *Hermit Songs* and another important American acquisition, Martha Graham's *El Penitente*. The programme cover, designed by Noberto Chiesa, who was to remain a valued designer for many years, bore the legend '1969 Year of The Place', but it also contained a most unhappy preface by Robin Howard:

> The Contemporary Ballet Trust was formed to give British contemporary dance of the highest possible standard. It seeks to do this by importing the very best from overseas to set the standard and to provide leadership whilst giving the maximum encouragement to young creative and performing artists. The aim was, and is, to develop a genuine British contemporary dance but not introverted. Whilst firmly rooted here it must remain international and continue to co-operate with the other arts and it must reflect the world outside.
>
> These aims are ambitious and in most ways we have been successful. Our School has become the leading European Centre of contemporary dance teaching; we have presented many new works by new choreographers, and our Group of five dancers has played to over 25,000 people throughout the British Isles.
>
> No company, however, can improve and develop properly without per-

Dinah Goodes in Robert Cohan's Shanta Quintet *(1969)*

forming and our Company has not performed since 1967. We are presenting this season, even though we still do not have the financial support we anticipated, partly because the Company is now ready for London, where it has never performed before, partly because, if we do not, our standards must decline and our dancers disperse.

The financial position of the Contemporary Ballet Trust is simple but sad. This building and the Artists' Place Society can continue without the Trust, but the Trust cannot without more money from somewhere. Our main donor has contributed all he can and unless more money is found by Christmas the Trust must close down. It is hard to believe that Britain cannot find at least as much money for its only contemporary dance organisation as it finds for eight or nine different classical ballet organisations, each of which on average, receives over five times as much as we do.

During the season, we are presenting dancers we have trained with others who are interested in performing regularly with us, in works by our Artistic Director, Robert Cohan, and by two first rate British choreographers contracted to us, Clover Roope and Barry Moreland, with three other works closely

*William Louther in Alvin
Ailey's* Hermit Songs, *first
staged by LCDT in 1969*

linked with us. Martha Graham is our Artistic Adviser; William Louther created the Alvin Ailey role he now dances with us, and Patricia Christopher choreographed *Reef* for our Company when teaching with us.

Next year, subject to money, we plan to give Company performances here in the Spring and Autumn. Our repertory will be the best works from this season with new works by Cohan, Roope and Moreland and, we hope, from our workshop performances. Works have also been promised by Ailey, Cunningham, Graham, Nikolais, and Taylor from America, by Cebron from Europe – and from Africa. Most of our Company will be the same as this season with the 'British' dancers taking on more important roles and being joined occasionally by some of our most promising students. Then we will have a real British Contemporary Dance Company with an international repertory, and the first stage of our development will be complete.

Up to the time of these performances we have received very little financial support, but many people have encouraged and helped us in other ways. We are most grateful to them all.

We are especially grateful to Lord Goodman, that near miracle worker, for all his help and encouragement and in showing his interest by opening The Place; to the Mayor of Camden, Dame Florence Cayford, for agreeing to be the first President of Artists' Place Society, and to the Deputy Mayor, Councillor A. W. Roome, for attending our opening performances. Finally, my personal thanks to everyone in the Contemporary Ballet Trust, especially to the dancers for accepting years of far too few performances and far too little money; to the American stars for being such stars on stage and only there, and especially to our Artistic Director, Robert Cohan. I challenge anyone to name one person in the world who is a better choreographer-performer-teacher-inspirer-explainer-leader-helper-bag carrier-floor sweeper and friend.

The opening programme for the season was a very strong one beginning with Cohan's *Side Scene*, to a selection of pre-classical music, with designs by Norberto Chiesa and featuring William Louther with Barry Moreland and three girls, Linda Gibbs, Dinah Goodes, and Xenia Hribar. This was followed by Graham's *El Penitente* of 1940, with music by Louis Horst and superlatively designed by Isamu Noguchi. Cohan had brought in his personal luggage the essential properties for the work: an apple and a cross, hand-carved by Noguchi and thus of considerable value.* The dance was given superb interpretation by Cohan as the Penitent, Louther as the Christ Figure and Noemi Lapzeson as the Virgin. The programme ended with Cohan's *Sky* to music by Eugene Lester, a long-time musical associate of Graham's.

The season was important also in that it brought the first two choreographies of Barry Moreland, *Cortège* and *Hosannas*, and an exceptionally vivid piece

Noemi Lapzeson
in El Penitente

---

*Cohan told the customs official 'I want to declare a set.' He was wondering whether to value it at $25,000 or $50,000 when the man said, after a cursory glance, 'Is that all it is? How much alchohol, how many cigarettes? Go through . . .'

by Cohan, *Cell*, whose view of a trapped and desperate community came to a stunning climax as the characters were seen flickering under a barrage of strobe lighting.

The press reception for this season was almost entirely enthusiastic. Richard Buckle in the *Sunday Times* wrote 'And so Lord Goodman opened The Place with a flourish on Tuesday and the London Contemporary Dance Company began its first season in its fine new home. Martha Graham, who has inspired in Robin Howard the amazing labours which are producing such shining results, was not present in the flesh, as six of her dancers were, but then, as Browning said, Never the time and The Place and the loved one altogether.' John Percival in *The Times* noted later in the season that 'Three out of four ballets in the London Contemporary Dance Company's programme at The Place last night were created specially for the company. In this way it will develop its own personality, which is fine, although some of the present works are clearly ephemeral.' Returning to the season a week after the opening Buckle wrote 'It is a cheering thought that, thanks to Robin Howard, who has sold hotels to pay for it, we have a modern dance company in this country into which Martha Graham's fine dancers can fit without destroying its balance; and although we can not expect to keep Graham dancers for ever, thanks to Howard's London School of Contemporary Dance, also housed at The Place, there will be a constant stream of young people following in their train.' Perhaps the most significant comment came later in the year, on 8 November, when a *Times* fourth leader noted that both The Place and Sadler's Wells Theatre (vacated at the beginning of the year when the opera company moved to the Coliseum) had found new identities:

> Apart from the benefit they bring to the other arts, Sadler's Wells Theatre and The Place have between them completely transformed the pattern of theatrical dance activity in London . . . The surprising thing is not only that so much has been achieved so quickly but that it has been done with hardly any expenditure of public money. If the work is to be consolidated and developed the Arts Council and the local authorities will sooner or later (one hopes sooner) have to dip into their pockets. At least, though, they can see before doing so that the need exists and that there will be value for money.

During this successful season Robin Howard produced a document which made predictions for the future and also highlighted the already obvious problems connected with the work of the School and of the Trust itself. 'By August 1969 the School had received students from twenty-seven countries and had supplied teachers to the Royal Academy of Dancing, to leading ballet schools and to seven foreign countries.' He went on to observe that the Company had already made a first foreign visit and a first London season, which had included works by Cohan and by the first choreographer to graduate from the Company's workshops, Barry Moreland. But under the heading 'finances' came the comment that

after a grant of £5,000 from the Arts Council, the Trust still had a deficit

William Louther and Linda Gibbs in Robert Cohan's Side Scene *(1969)*

*Robert Powell and Noemi
Lapzeson in Robert Cohan's
Cell (1969)*

last year of £6,335. This was covered by a loan from a member of the Council which will be paid off by November 1, 1969. Ten year forward projections will be revised at the end of the September and available at the end of October. The most notable parts of the present projections are:

1. the more the School grows the less its deficits
2. the more the Company performs the greater its deficits
3. the more all the Trust's work grows the greater is the need and demand for experiment by the young creators
4. both School and Company are likely to receive sufficient income from fees, tickets and the State by September 1971 to be effectively self-supporting.

. . . At present the Trust is unable to meet the demand for teachers from other schools, but by September 1971 there should be 20 contemporary dance teachers in the London School and elsewhere in Britain . . . The Trust's School and Company are already the leaders of contemporary dance in Europe. With The Place as a headquarters offering such opportunities for co-operation between the arts, the prospects are immense.

These brave words were to receive a dreadful counterblast of financial reality by the end of the year, despite the fact that the demonstration group continued its tours (and also visited the Royal Ballet School), and despite an extraordinary first collaboration with Peter Maxwell Davies's Pierrot Players when, in December, William Louther choreographed and danced in *Vesalii Icones*. This was rightly hailed as a remarkable realisation of the religious themes of Maxwell Davies's score, in which Louther gave a performance of genius. In December, however, Robin Howard was forced to threaten disbandment. A press conference had been arranged to mark the moment when Howard signed a lease on The Place. As the signing was to take place, David Reynolds from the Arts Council handed Robin Howard a letter with the advice that he should 'read it at once'. It was a rejection of Howard's request for an increase in funding.

There seemed no way out of this problem. Howard took the chance and signed, and at the end of the season had to tell the Company that there would be no further money after December, his only request to them being to ask them to keep going for as long as possible while the Trust could provide even nominal maintenance. On 22 December, however, Robin Howard received a telephone call from Alexander Dunbar, Director of the Gulbenkian Foundation in the UK, promising that if Howard could maintain operations until April, the Foundation would then provide funding in the region of £30,000 over a period of three years. The next day Howard also received a call from John Cruft, Head of Music at the Arts Council, announcing that from 1 April 1970 an increased grant would be available. Thus it came about that as 1969 drew to a close the company was effectively disbanded, but would be reborn with the New Year. The Place and the company were reprieved and it has been the proud boast of the Trust that ever since April 1970 the dancers have been on fifty-two-week contracts.

William Louther in his own Vesalii Icones *(1970)*

1970

◆

The rebirth of activities in April 1970 was marked by the increase of the Arts Council grant to £20,000, and the first part of the generous Gulbenkian benefaction. As a witness of things to come, G. B. L. Wilson recorded in the *Dancing Times* of March of that year, after an informal visit to The Place, 'I saw a notice on the board, thus: "CONTRACTS – to make it sort of official, I record that we agreed . . . signed Robin".' The notice epitomised the unorthodox attitude towards formalities, and also the sense of total trust between dancers and director.

As the company prepared for its second London season in May and June the Trust presented a series of workshops. In *The Times* John Percival gave early testimony to the creative urge to be found in the Trust's programme.

> Nowadays, all our dance companies have some system for giving aspiring choreographers a chance, but I know no other organisation that goes to the same lengths as the London Contemporary Dance Theatre and its affiliated School to find and develop creative talent. Not only are the professional dancers encouraged to produce ballets, but all the students are actually required to do so as part of their training.
>
> Lately I have watched quite a few of these at The Place, in circumstances ranging from studio performances of work in progress, through 'open workshops' of selected pieces before an audience in the main theatre, to a special fund-raising performance yesterday. Obviously the standard varies a lot. Most of them are never meant to be shown publicly; what the choreographer and dancers can learn from their experience is the whole point. But the most encouraging thing about the venture is that even the unsuccessful works seem mostly to have a genuine idea behind them, either of theme or movement.

Among the works seen in these performances were the first choreographic essays of the American choreographer Flora Cushman, a significant creator and teacher, and head of the workshop programme in these early days, and of the young student Richard Alston who had joined the School in Berners Place. In an interview in *Dance and Dancers* (June 1978) Alston recalled these apprentice times: 'I made my first piece after studying for nine months. In those days the workshops were entirely undelineated; you would find yourself working with somebody like Noemi Lapzeson although one was only a first year student; anyone could choose anyone to work with since they were just feverishly looking for choreographers.'

Noemi Lapzeson and Robert North in Paul Taylor's Duet, *first staged by LCDT in 1970*

The second London season took place between 27 May and 14 June. The opening programme comprised Graham's *El Penitente*, with William Louther as the Penitent and Robert North making his first mark in a major role with the Company as the Christ figure, and Noemi Lapzeson as the woman. It was followed by a new work from Louther, *Divertissement: In the Playground of the Zodiac*, and concluded with a revival of *Cell*, in which Robert Powell repeated his tense, fiercely edgy and most moving performance.

The subsequent repertory brought Robert North's *Conversation Piece*; Cohan's *Eclipse* and *Hunter of Angels*; *Gourami*, a short duet by Jack Nightingale; Richard Alston's *Something to Do*; Flora Cushman's *Raga Shankara*; Alvin Ailey's *Hermit Songs*, again miraculously danced by William Louther; two works by Paul Taylor, *Duet* and *Three Epitaphs*; and Barry Moreland's *Hosannas* and *Nocturnal Dances*. The scope of the repertory was already impressive and the fact that The Place had provided a home for Peter Maxwell Davies's Pierrot Players had encouraged the fascinating collaborations of *Nocturnal Dances* and *Vesalii Icones*.

In an introduction to the season's programme, Robin Howard could state with pride that the Trust's work had culminated, over seven years, in twelve dancers in the Company trained by the School and eleven works produced by seven choreographers. He noted that 'All full time students have their first class in dance composition at the beginning of their first term. Between September and January students, staff and Company members produced over 40 new works – some only short studies – and this summer will see another 40. In three years time we should be producing over 20 ballets a year worthy of showing to the public, some conventional and some experimental. In three years time, too, we shall be ten years old. If ten years later our standards and our creativity are still rising then those of us who were in at the beginning will feel that our policy was right.'

As some justification for Robin Howard's optimism it is worth recording that the season was so successful that it was extended by seven days from the dates originally announced.

After the London season the pattern of touring was re-established, taking the Company around Britain and into Europe. In Oxford on 24 July Robert Cohan's *X* was given its first performance. This was a work dealing, like *Cell*, with the fears and tensions of a group of people who seemed to find relief in smoking pot. Peter Williams in *Dance and Dancers* felt that it treated the combatting of the fear that had earlier been explored in *Cell*.

After two weeks holiday the Company embarked on its first important foreign tour, visiting Yugoslavia, Czechoslovakia and Italy betwen 25 August and 11 September. The Company was admired by its new audiences, and Robin Howard noted particularly the effect on the dancers of finding a large theatre enthusiastically applauding them, as compared with the far smaller numbers they knew at the far smaller Place. It was ironic, perhaps, to note that when, on the com-

Robert Cohan's X (1971) *with Robert North and Bob Smith on the right and Michelene McKnight in profile.*

pany's return to Britain it was invited to appear at the Windsor Festival, and danced in the Farrer Theatre in Eton College, the local newspaper recorded that 'a disappointingly small audience' only really warmed to the dancers after Paul Taylor's *Three Epitaphs*.

The Company's third season at The Place was scheduled for 13–25 October and was no less successful than earlier London showings. William Louther and Noemi Lapzeson led a company which numbered seventeen dancers, many of whom were to be influential and long-term members of the troupe – Linda Gibbs, Clare Duncan, Xenia Hribar and Sue (Siobhan) Davies, Robert North, Micha Bergese and Norman Murray (Namron). London was given the opportunity of seeing *X* for the first time, along with a new work by Barry Moreland, the charming *Summer Games*, which had previously been shown in workshop performance, while the company also acquired a piece by the Dutch choreographer Pauline de Groot. This was *Rainmakers*, which did little for its cast, and prompted the opinion of the *Financial Times* that it was 'as ineffective as it is dull, since not a drop of rain has fallen since it was performed'.

Robin Howard, ever concerned with the identity and the functions of the Trust, made a series of comments in the season's programme and an appeal.

The workshops continue to develop choreographers and dancers and the School continues to expand – it has just had a record intake of new full time students. In short, the Trust's three operational units are now developing nearly as planned. The Contemporary Ballet Trust, which controls the operational units at The Place, has spent much of the last six months in trying to raise money, reviewing its administration and re-defining its objectives. General suggestions made during our discussions have included:

1. our Trust's policy is based on three things: quality, enterprise and love

2. we should make every effort to play our full part in the life of Camden

3. whilst remaining an artistic organisation we must at times comment upon moral and social problems

4. we must find the right way to use the universal language of dance to break down social, political, linguistic and other barriers

5. contemporary dance is in no way in competition with classical ballet either in its history or approach. It is something different. If this form of dance is necessary to the British dance scene it should be subsidised accordingly

6. it should be based in London

7. its standards should never, for any reason, be allowed to decline

And for the Place it has been suggested:

8. The Place should become more a home for the Dance Theatre and the School and less of a general arts centre

9. we should have more Brunch Concerts and through them create a forum for young artists in any media

In October of 1970 the School was recognised by the Inner London Education Authority for the acceptance of grant-aided students, part of the gradual process of recognition which allowed students to apply for study grants, and by November the merits of the School's work were being increasingly revealed to public approval. On 1 November a Brunch Concert was given at the The Place, where for 12s 6d an audience received a light meal and a drink (either fruit juice or, for hardier souls, a Bloody Mary) and was then able to watch a lecture demonstration which allowed students and apprentice members of the Company to perform in front of an audience. At this first concert the speaker was Richard Alston, who introduced a display of Graham technique and then joined Maria Casey, Sue Davies and Ritva Lehtinen in his *Nowhere Slowly*. On 17 and 24 November Robert Cohan and Flora Cushman, Director of the workshop programme, presented two evenings of new works. The first performance brought creations by Noemi Lapzeson, Robert North, Barry Moreland and Franca Telesio (all members of the Company), Ruth Posner (a teacher at the School), and Christopher Banner, a third-year student. The second evening featured choreographies by Flora Cushman, Xenia Hribar, Richard Alston, Rebecca Wilson, and Catherine Lewis, another third-year student.

Linda Gibbs in Barry Moreland's Summer Games *(1970)*

1971

◆

Nineteen seventy-one began with the company already installed at The Place for a six-week season which had begun on 30 December. The repertory was still expanding, with new works by Barry Moreland (*The Troubadors*), Noemi Lapzeson (*Cantabile*, her first choreography), Richard Alston (his *Nowhere Slowly*, with a new Stockhausen score – 'for consenting piano' declared Richard Buckle – replacing the Terry Riley music that had been used for its Workshop appearance in November), and Flora Cushman, whose *Raga Shankara* was joined by *Macroseconds*, originally created for her students at Dartington. Robert Cohan made *Consolation of the Rising Moon* for the company and the acquisition of Talley Beatty's *Road of the Phoebe Snow* brough the bravura demands for American jazz dance into the dancers' experience.

Not all these novelties could be considered successful, but they testify to the creativity that so strongly marked these early days. The company could proudly quote Noël Goodwin's comment in the *Daily Express* that 'Existing trends of modern and future dance are being charted in a way that has no previous parallel in this country.' Audiences were reacting with delight to the developing skills of the company's dancers, not least in their ability to meet the challenges of *Phoebe Snow*'s explosion of jazz energy. The ballet had been previously seen in London with the Alvin Ailey company; William Louther repeated the role of the hero he had danced with Ailey to sensational effect, and Linda Gibbs emerged as a dancer of power and beauty as the girl who is raped and falls onto the track of the eponymous railway train.

The season continued to evince favourable comment from the press, Nigel Gosling declaring in the *Observer* that no other company in Britain could compete with the creativity of the London Dance Theatre Company. 'New works fall from it thick and fast, many of them spin-offs from the troupe's frequent workshop experiments.' The standard of design was also admired in the press. It should be stated that, from the very first, Robert Cohan (who was also to work pseudonymously as the designer Charter) had sought to show an elegance of manner in presentation and a clarity in lighting which were almost unknown to other British dance companies at this time. We record with gratitude that this tradition has been handsomely maintained through subsequent years, and this design attitude can be understood as part of Cohan's inheritance from Martha Graham and from the American theatre's appreciation of how dancing can be enhanced by stage lighting. Certainly the contribution of Peter Farmer as

Noemi Lapzeson, Robert North and Celeste Dandeker in Cantabile *(1970). Photograph by Frederika Davis*

55

a designer during these early years was of real significance in helping to give the company its visual identity. In this early 1971 season he had provided the decoration for six works in the repertory, furnishing bare and beautiful settings and opulent Persian-style costuming for Cohan's *Consolation of the Rising Moon* and for Robert North's *Conversation Piece*, and witty outfits for Noemi Lapzeson's *Cantabile*.

In discussing the work of the School as a nursery for The Place's future, Robin Howard could at this time be confident that many local authorities were prepared to offer grants to suitable students, and that the School's attendance figures indicated the ever-widening appeal of contemporary dance: 'There are 53 students doing a full time three year course (32 in their first year) and ten doing a special one year course, with over 150 regular part time students including children and teenage classes.'

The general public's awareness of the Trust's work was enhanced by the Company's own touring, by its lecture demonstrations and its continued participation in Ballet for All's programmes. Ballet for All's *On With the Dance* was a typical 'ballet play' devised by Peter Brinson which contrasted the different ideals of ballet and the Graham style, and helped win a new audience through the participation of young dancers from the Royal Ballet and from the London Contemporary Dance ensemble.

Another boost to public awareness of the Trust's work came with the BBC's transmission on 8 January 1971 of *Lifelines*, an eighteen-minute dance piece specially created for television by Cohan. With a score by Ronald Lloyd, who had composed the accompaniment to *Cell*, it dealt with a young woman reliving the delights and sorrows of a love affair.

In a round-up comment on the season at the The Place, Peter Brinson wrote in the *Times Educational Supplement* that performances had shown 'how mature the company has grown and how real is the alternative it now offers to the classical style maintained at Covent Garden. Barely two years ago, in 1969, the Arts Council's report on opera and ballet noted the "rapidly growing interest and appreciation of contemporary dance, especially among young people", so that "the future development of the London Contemporary Dance Group and Company should be watched carefully and considered seriously".'

The Arts Council itself in its *Bulletin* for Spring 1971 declared that LCDT 'is now established as a most valuable addition to the pattern of British Ballet.'

There emerged at this time another element to help take contemporary dance to a wider public. This was the X Group – 'X' standing for Experimental – made up of students in their final period of study at the School who toured round colleges and educational centres, under the direction of Flora Cushman, with a repertory which also included student works. The message was clear: creativity was the Trust's watchword.

A triumphant affirmation of what LCDT stood for in matters of artistic enterprise was provided in April of this year with the production of Robert Cohan's

William Louther and Linda Gibbs in Talley Beatty's The Road of the Phoebe Snow, *first staged by LCDT in 1971*

Stages. This was certainly the boldest and most expensive undertaking so far, a two-act modern dance work whose effects – from multi-level production to Kirby's Flying Ballet, by way of gymnastics and every trick of mixed-media presentation – stretched the resources of The Place and its artists to the full. Among other innovations, *Stages* involved the reversing of theatre and auditorium by seating the public on what was customarily the stage area and using the four levels of tiered seating as the performing area for both dancers and musicians. The result was dazzling, a virtuoso exercise in production and choreography which brought credit to Cohan, to his dancers and to Peter Farmer as designer. It gripped its audience from the first and did not let them go until an explosion brought the set crashing in ruins round the cast in a final *coup de théâtre*.

The work was sub-titled 'An Impression in Two Parts of a Heromyth'. Its theme was a spiritual journey which brought its protagonist face to face with his essential self. The hero was portrayed by William Louther, and both Cohan and the public were fortunate to have an artist of such heroic power, both technical and emotional, as the focal point of the action. In the first act the hero descends into a grey and nightmarish underworld by means of a splendid theatrical trick: Louther drifted downwards amid the flicker of strobe lighting like an angel in a Cocteau film. There he met with the macabre denizens of this region and a multi-imaged goddess figure, superbly portrayed by Noemi Lapzeson. Screens and ramps enabled Peter Farmer to transform the four levels of the usual seating area and John B. Read's lighting was a powerful aid to the illusion of this first section. To an electronic score by Arne Nordheim, Louther journeyed through suffering and temptation, came face to face with his own image, was tortured in interrogation and moved on to the second part of the work with a burden of experience which would prove of little use to him. The second act was set in a modern world of glaring colours and vicious pop imagery and sustained by a raucously efficient score from Bob Downes.

There followed a succession of dream confrontations with his own self and with various monsters, until a final freak-out of lurid psychedelic vitality held him in this Pilgrim's Progress. But the Hero moved through all this until, at the work's end, a blinded and agonised Samson, he tore down two silver pillars that surmounted the set, leaving behind him total destruction as he walked out of the theatre beneath a flashing Exit sign.

Stages was an extraordinary work, remarkable both in its pace and in its theatrical vitality. The choreography achieved almost hallucinatory effects and the dancing of the cast was exemplary. The various elements – gymnastics (in which the cast were coached by Pauline Prestidge of the National Olympic Team), film, a constantly shifting stage area – all contributed to the general theme and made its every allusion clear, while Peter Farmer's design showed what extraordinary things were possible even in the unpromising surroundings of a small theatre. For Louther there can not be praise enough. He was an artist who gave

Stages *by Robert Cohan (1971)*
with Noemi Lapzeson in Part I

William Louther in Robert Cohan's Consolation of the Rising Moon, *1971*

London Contemporary Dance in these early years impeccable technique and impeccable artistry, and his greatness as a dancer and that indefinable star quality which he possessed illuminated the repertory and inspired public and colleagues alike.

The importance of *Stages* was to become even clearer in the following year when it proved a tremendous box office draw for the new audiences the company was to meet on its extended regional tours.

The summer brought the arrival of Jane Dudley, initially to teach on a Summer Course at the School. An eminent dancer with Graham, and dancer-choreographer with the adventurous Dudley/Maslow/Bales New Dance company, in taking up residence in London to work at The Place she was a vital adjunct to the teaching staff, bringing the integrity of main-stream Graham technique to the students and young dancers of the Company.

In this summer, too, LCDT embarked upon another European tour which took them first to the Festival du Marais in Paris between 7–14 June.*

There followed a short visit to Switzerland, most notable for the fact that it was here that Robert Cohan danced his last performance with the company. He had been suffering from back pain and during a performance of *El Penitente* he found himself thinking 'I don't have to dance any more'. The idea came with no sense of personal regret. For twenty-five years he had been one of the great performers of his generation and could justifiably feel that there was no further technical peaks he wished to scale. His decision to retire from performing meant that he could concentrate all his energies upon the life of the company and upon creativity – there were great challenges ahead.

On their return to Britain, LCDT undertook a regional tour but by October the company was again in Europe, visiting Czechoslovakia and Poland for a British Council tour and, for the first time, showing in the Eastern bloc the most adventurous choreography Britain could offer. The reaction everywhere was admiring, one Swiss critic remarking that 'One thing is sure: the London Contemporary Dance Theatre we have just seen is near perfect in the modern style.' The same critic, Germaine Soullier, made a comment that would be repeated by many other foreign observers: that the LCDT dancers gave themselves wholly to their art. The sense of dedication in these early performances has run like a grain through the entire history of the company.

*Janet Eager, as Administrator of the company, was paid on the last day of the Paris visit. In cash. Banks proved unwilling to accept all this currency and to get it out of France, Janet Eager was obliged to secrete it about her person. She astutely stood in line at customs behind the loveliest girl in the company, who inevitably caught the eye of the Customs official while 'Mop' Eager and the money walked through unchallenged.

1972

◆

Following this Eastern bloc visit the company returned for appearances in Bath and Brighton before embarking on a rehearsal period as prelude to another London season. The triumph of *Stages* meant, inevitably, that this featured in the first two weeks of the season which began on 11 January 1972 at The Place. The opening performance was not untouched by drama. The leading role of the hero was due to be taken for the first time by Robert Powell, who had earlier been a guest star with the Company. He was taken ill, and seven hours before curtain rise William Louther, now an associate artist with LCDT, was called upon to replace him in the slightly revised text of the piece. A few days later Powell was able to appear as the hero and played magnificently, his reading characterised by that expressive clarity which marked all his dancing. 'The Place in Duke's Road, Euston', wrote Mary Clarke in the *Guardian*, 'is sold out for the two weeks of repertory with which London Contemporary Dance Theatre is following two sold out weeks of Robert Cohan's *Stages*. But it is worth trying for returns: the company is in terrific form.' The repertory included Anna Sokolow's *Scenes from the Music of Charles Ives*, which she had lately staged for the dancers of the Juilliard School in New York, and this featured another exceptional performance by Robert Powell ('Nobody who danced as Robert Powell did on Wednesday,' observed Richard Buckle in the *Sunday Times*, 'could be said to have danced in vain.')

There were also four pieces that had originally been tried out in the company's workshop performances: Xenia Hribar's *Some Dream*, *One Was The Other*, jointly made by Robert North and Noemi Lapzeson, Richard Alston's *Cold* and Barry Moreland's *Kontakion*. *Cold* was remarkable in that it was set to part of Adolphe Adam's score for the second act of *Giselle*, and these Romantic strains in the home of modern dance attracted much comment. In the *Financial Times* Andrew Porter commented: 'It is not just a parody: that would be too easy to be entertaining. But rather, a composition in which episodes of the Coralli/Petipa work are used, placed, framed, set out for inspection, in the course of a dance that is freely and fluently composed on ideas from its original.' Porter also suggested that *Kontakion* had one especial advantage: 'Someone who writes a dance work with William Louther in the leading role can hardly go wrong. A mystery play on the life of Christ is bound in almost any circumstances to make its effect. But without trying to determine how much Barry Moreland owes to his interpreters, and how much to a scenario whose scenes and imagery

Robert North in One Was the Other, *which he choreographed with Noemi Lapzeson (1972)*

63

permeate Western culture, we can praise *Kontakion* as a moving and powerful exercise . . . Mr Louther transfigures whatever he touches; in his Christ there burns a shining, dedicated flame.' (It is good to record that *Kontakion*, with Louther, was later to be recorded by Thames TV and subsequently won a prize at the International TV Festival in Salzburg.)

Immediately prior to this season Robin Howard produced a letter for members of The Place Society, who provided much-needed and consistent support for all the activities at The Place. Talking of the School with its then current enrolment of eighty-five full-time students and more than 200 part-time pupils, Howard noted:

> Only in the last eighteen months have students with such a full training started joining the Company, first Siobhan Davies, then Celeste Dandeker, and Paula Lansley. All first performed here at The Place before becoming full Company members, just as Anthony van Laast and Stephen Barker are now doing. The Company gave its first London performances in September 1969, but it was not until April 1970 that we were able to offer the dancers a full year's employment. By the beginning of March 1972, the Dance Theatre will have given twice as many performances as in the previous year and have completed two foreign tours, one in France and Switzerland, and one to Czechoslovakia and Poland. These tours were particularly exciting: after The Place it is quite an experience to appear in a packed 2,000 seat opera house and receive standing ovations with rhythmical handclaps. At first we had to build up a basic repertory and rely very heavily on our star dancers. This season we are lucky still to have three such dancers with us; one, William Louther, appears as our first associated artist but the other Company members now have leading roles and we have double cast nearly all our basic repertory.
>
> Choreographically, we continue a policy of encouraging our own people, but bringing in guests when we think it necessary and, far more to the point, when we can afford it. This season we are proud to present the British premiere of a new work by Anna Sokolow, the great American choreographer, along with four new productions from our own Workshops. In fact our current repertory is home-grown except for the three works by Miss Sokolow, Talley Beatty and Paul Taylor.

A further incentive to creativity came in April, when the Gulbenkian Foundation announced the first two grants of its dance-commissioning programme. Coincidentally they went to the same choreographer, Remy Charlip, who was to create a new piece for LCTD and a youth work for Scottish Ballet.

As a prelude to the May season at The Place the dancers of the X Group appeared for one night, dancing in St Pancras Church, which stands immediately opposite The Place and was then celebrating its 150th year. Its chimes can still be heard ringing through The Place and through performances in the theatre every quarter of an hour. (On certain dreadful evenings this has proved the happiest way of ticking off the passage of time.)

Siobhan Davies in Barry Moreland's Kontakion *(1972). Photograph by Helen Leoussi*

64

Richard Alston's Cold *(1972)*

The season began on 16 May and was originally designed to feature a major new piece for each week. The programme began with Remy Charlip's *Dance*, was to continue with Robert Cohan's *People* and Flora Cushman's briefer *Scalene Sequence*, and finish with *Combines*, Richard Alston's most ambitious work to date. Charlip's *Dance* was, as Andrew Porter wrote 'not so much dancing as about dancing, and about the way that every movement made, or even thought about, can be thought of as a dance. "Typing is a dance; taking a bath is a dance; a laugh is a dance; talking is a song you can dance to; a caress is a dance; a signature is a name dance." *Tutto nel mondo e ballo* . . . Fine, if you can see and feel the world that way. And fine of Remy Charlip to have shown us that for a while it can be so.'

Despite the evident charm of the idea, and the very considerable charm of the performers as they mimed and danced and painted and fulfilled suggestions for movement called out by the audience (one less than enchanted viewer requested that they should dance), *Dance* was thin on the very thing that it proclaimed in its title. It was innocent, open-hearted and fatally twee.

During the first week of *Dance* a gala was held at The Place in aid of student scholarships. All the seats were priced at £5.00 (all the sightlines in that theatre are perfect) and it was hoped to raise £1,000. In the event that sum was exceeded by £500.

But by now a very serious problem had emerged, boding ill for the continuation of the season: Robert Cohan had become ill, and the planned new work *People* had to be cancelled. Additional performances of *Dance* filled in the gap in the programming. In the final week, however, Alston's *Combines* reasserted the adventurous nature of Place creativity. The Place itself, said Andrew Porter 'had all the atmosphere that the BBC Round House concerts miss. (It also has a better restaurant, a more efficient bar, and a welcome.) The feel is right for an evening of enjoyment. Half-conquered before the evening has begun, we sit in surroundings that enhance what is good, make us tolerant of what (occasionally) may be dull. The current double bill is not dull at all.'

The double bill began with Flora Cushman's *Scalene Sequence*, developed from an early workshop piece, which was a trio for Anca Frankenhaeuser (still a student), Christopher Banner and Anthony van Laast, in which Van Laast was the dominant figure. The second piece, *Combines*, found Richard Alston seeking to bridge the gap between filmed dance and stage movement. It was episodic in nature and used a musical collage of Schubert, Bach and Chopin. Its chief merit was that the personalities of its cast, which included Stephen Barker, Micha Bergese, Celeste Dandeker, Siobhan Davies, Anthony van Laast, Paula Lansley and Ross McKim, came over very strongly.

After this London showing the company went on the road and for the first time was able to tour *Stages*, which had its regional premiere in the University Theatre at Newcastle upon Tyne on 25 July (tickets cost 40p, 60p, 70p and 80p). At the same time the X Group gave its first public season in London in the

Open Air Theatre of Holland Park, following hard on the heels of the students of the Royal Ballet School who had just given a summer week of performances. The programme included two pieces by Flora Cushman: *Outshoulder* was 'an easy opener; the dancers are warming up and it doesn't matter when you arrive. It is a dance for two men, three girls and a step ladder – and when they have finished the dancers just pack up and go. The closing *Scalene Sequence* is more formally constructed. The music, by Kabelac and Berio, is compulsive and the closing virtuoso solo by Anthony van Laast is so compelling that the audience did not even notice the rain that began to fall gently towards its end.' So wrote Mary Clarke in the *Guardian*.

London Contemporary Dance's next London season came in high summer when the company joined the *ICES 72* Festival. This was a celebration of avant-garde music, an International Carnival of Experimental Sound held between 13 and 26 August at The Round House and The Place. The first dance in the Festival came, most significantly, as an experimental break-away from LCDT itself. This was the appearance of Richard Alston's new company, Strider, on 14 August at The Place. It marked the first necessary development of contemporary dance away from the apron strings of The Trust and both Robin Howard and Robert Cohan welcomed this adventure. Here was the proof that after just five years talent was abundant and seeking its own different voice.

On 16 August LCDT began its participation in this Carnival, and a profusion of new work was again in evidence: Flora Cushman's *Gamma Garden*, Ross McKim's *Tearful History*, Stephen Barker's *Fugue?*, Xenia Hribar's *Treeo*, *Outside-In* by Anthony van Laast and Micha Bergese, Christopher Banner's *Afar*, Richard Alston's *Tiger Balm* (also seen with Strider), Noemi Lapzeson's *Conundrum*, and a first professional piece by Siobhan Davies, *Relay*.

From the ICES Festival the company moved into a week's season at The Place on 29 August, which brought the initial performances of *People Alone*. This was the first part of what had been intended as a full-length work dealing with the isolation of various characters. The original intention had been that each member of the cast would create a situation for a dance concerned with loneliness, which Robert Cohan would then shape into an overall text. As Peter Williams wrote in *Dance and Dancers*, 'It should have been the centrepiece of the London Contemporary Dance Theatre's early summer season. It had to be scrapped because Cohan became ill. Most of the pieces by the company were re-thought and shown either in workshop or other programmes. The nature of Cohan's illness was lengthy and depressive, with many lonely hours for his mind to mull around his own worries and those of his company. During this time the nature of *People* changed considerably and what was finally shown was a work entirely by Cohan with a commissioned score by Bob Downes, and a part of what will eventually become a full length piece.'

The printed programme for this season also kept the work of the Trust before the public eye. It listed the activities of the School under Patricia Hutchinson

Mackenzie, identified Jane Dudley as Director of Graham Studies and also announced that 'full time students' classes include Dance Composition with Nina Fonaroff – dancer and teacher with Martha Graham and choreographer for her own company in New York where she has been teaching for the past twelve years; music with Judyth Knight who has been associated with the Trust for many years; and design with Norberto Chiesa who designed settings for Cohan's *Cell* and *People Alone* . . . Choreographic Workshops are an integral part of training and life at The Place, starting from within the School, and continuing to the X Group and the Dance Theatre.'

The work of the X Group fulfilled an important role between the School and the Dance Theatre: 'Providing experience and opportunity for young dancers and choreographers prior to joining the main company, and as an experimental group, it is designed to perform the types of work rarely presented by larger companies, for organisations unable to accommodate a large company.' With no trace of vainglory, LCDT could boast that its policy of encouraging young choreographers in this country had meant that already in 1972 it had presented fifteen new works, ten of which were choreographed by its own members. By Christmas, there would be four more new works in the repertory, including a new piece by Robert North which was to have its first performance in Bath in October, during a week of repertory. North's *Brian* was a study in madness. North presented his public with the disparate elements of his hero's plight and, after the fashion of a jigsaw, gradually fitted the pieces together into a portrait. Excellently staged – Peter Owen's set comprised three revolving panels which made up a screen that could be variously decorated – and excellently danced by North and Stephen Barker as two halves of a schizoid personality, it brought Linda Gibbs as the Oedipal figure of the wife/mother in a work which was more an illustration to a spoken text than a dance piece, but markedly effective for all that.

A summing up of the company's progress thus far came in an important interview which Robert Cohan gave to James Monahan (writing as James Kennedy) in the *Guardian*:

A school, a home theatre, a permanent company, a distinctive home-grown repertory – these in the past five years have been Cohan's necessities just as in the 'thirties they were a necessity for Dame Ninette de Valois; and now, at The Place, he has acquired a school, a theatre and company and the home-grown repertory is on the way. When the Sadler's Wells Ballet began Dame Ninette was, perforce, its chief choreographer; either she herself had to make ballets or the repertory would have consisted entirely of borrowings from the international past.

Similarly, Mr Cohan since 1967 has made twelve works for his company and, for the rest, has taken what he could get from the previous choreography of Graham, Alvin Ailey, Paul Taylor and other Americans. But the CDT is now beginning to produce its own choreography and Mr Cohan hopes that

Robert North and Ross McKim in Richard Alston's Tiger Balm *(1972). Photograph by Colin Clarke*

Robert Cohan's People Alone *with (left to right) Celia Hulton, Sally Estep, Anita Griffin, Philippe Giraudeau and Christopher Bannerman (1972)*

in two or three years its choreography, apart from some of the modern classics from America, will be its very own. That is his target. In the meantime the CDT has survived the worst of the financial difficulties which beset it, mainly because the School which used to consume a lot of the £40,000 to £50,000 available in grants has now become self-supporting.

Another sort of financial difficulty remains: the market for dancers (as Mr Cohan told me) is so voracious that already American modern dance companies are trying to take away his London trained students; apart from that it is quite impossible for the CDT to pay its members the sort of wages offered to dancers by the commercial theatre. It is only dedication which keeps dancers at The Place.

The greater part of LCDT's autumn tour was devoted to taking *Stages* around the regions with Robert North and Micha Bergese admirably cast as the hero. *Stages* proved to be a block-busting success. Stanley Reynolds (reporting from Liverpool for the *Guardian*) provided a brilliant commentary upon the whole evening and ended with the comment 'It is a superb, triumphant and absolutely exhilarating evening. And, thank God, it played last night in Liverpool to a capacity house at the Royal Court, which clapped like thunder, stamped its feet and whistled through its teeth for more.'

In preparation for its end of the year season at The Place, LCDT had invited May O'Donnell to teach and to mount a work. May O'Donnell, one of Graham's finest artists from as far back as the 1930s, decided to stage her *Dance Energies* for the company, an entirely new piece in which she sought to explore the vitality and youthful power of the dancers. The choreography was somewhat diffuse and uneven in its components but it provided an essential link with the bloodlines of the Graham company and Graham technique.

The other novelty of the season was Lotte Goslar's *Ends and Odds*. A student of Wigman and Gret Palucca in Germany, Goslar had worked significantly in America in the theatre and as a dancer-mime. *Ends and Odds* was designed for the young and proved to be tremendous fun, involving a children's audience without patronising them. The piece was ideal entertainment at matinees over the Christmas holidays for parents and children, not least in its audience participation and in a gently charming sequence set to Schubert Waltzes and beautifully danced by Celeste Dandeker and Micha Bergese.

And thus, as the year ended, LCDT could list a repertory provided by eleven choreographers, eight of whom were members of the organisation. After only three years of professional existence this was an astounding achievement.

1973

◆

The year 1973 began for LCDT as it did for the nation with the *Fanfare for Europe* festivities connected with Britain's entry into the Common Market. The Royal Ballet, London Festival Ballet and Scottish Ballet staged celebratory galas and, not to be outdone, LCDT on 11, 12 and 13 January brought back *Stages* into the repertory at The Place with Micha Bergese as the hero, Robert North as the brooding figure of his experience, and Noemi Lapzeson as the goddess. The production had been slightly revised by Cohan and now achieved what was to be its final form; taut, hallucinatory, a 'bad trip' in Cocteau country as the *Financial Times* called it, and stunningly effective. It played, not surprisingly, to sold-out houses.

As the printed programme for the season noted:

The Dance Theatre has another season only five weeks after this one finishes, as the Camden Festival is earlier this year. Robert Cohan will be choreographing a new work, and as children's matinees have proved so popular, it hoped to arrange at least two special performances in early March. A short spring tour includes the Oxford Playhouse, April 2–7, as well as Malvern and Norwich, then the company starts a seven week tour of South America for the British Council. Before returning home they will give three performances at Connecticut College, Conn., USA.*

The new Cohan work scheduled to feature in the Camden Festival was commissioned with funds provided by the Arts Council. *People Together* was the pendant and second part of *People Alone*. Peter Williams, as usual, reviewed it very perceptively in *Dance and Dancers*:

It was expected I think that Robert Cohan would follow 'all the lonely people' of his *People Alone* with something about people who love people being the luckiest people in the world. That is what the title of the new piece, *People Together*, would seem to imply. But Cohan, in a programme note for the work that completes the diptych under the collective title *People* says 'that people together seem to be more alone than people alone' or that's what he has discovered from observing human behaviour. It is a sad but alas perfectly realistic reflection of our time that with the massing and huddling that goes

*This visit to Connecticut College did not in fact take place.

Robert Cohan's Mass (1973)

on – in the playgrounds for all ages, in pop festivals, in protest demonstrations, and even in mass religious manifestations – all this only increases the inner solitude of the individual.

The Camden Festival season also brought another gala in aid of student grants on 9 March, but it was during this early part of the year that a possibility arose that the Trust might leave Camden. A golden opportunity was presented to Robin Howard with the chance of new premises, a new theatre and generous local council funding. The old Lyric Theatre, Hammersmith, much loved and much used, had fallen victim to redevelopment. It had been razed to the ground in the early seventies and on its site was proposed a new ultra-modern theatre of medium size. The site developers were willing to make an important capital contribution and Hammersmith Council would provide further massive funding with additional subsidies anticipated from the Greater London Council and the Arts Council. Here, it was suggested, the Trust would find a new home, new studios and a theatre which could support a wide variety of entertainment. Robin Howard was photographed on the site; local and international identity was planned for the enterprise, and a feasibility study went happily forward. In the event, despite every aspiration, the funding of the enterprise was to prove impossible and The Place remained the company's home, though further problems about the tenancy of the Duke's Road site were to loom in the not-too-distant future.

After the Camden Festival, the Dance Theatre once again took the road, to give the first performance in Oxford of Cohan's latest work *Mass*, which was the fruit of a seven-month collaboration with the composer Vladimir Rodzianko. It was a more than usually complex collaboration between composer and choreographer in that the dancers were both vocalists and performers. Pre-recorded tapes formed a musical basis that was embellished by chanting, cries and recitation by the cast of part of the text of the Mass. This produced the immediacy of expression that was Cohan's first concern: for him the word Mass had not only a sacramental meaning but also a deeper linguistic identity concerning a group of people. The religious connotation was obscured by the actuality of the performance; the work was less a prayer for the dead than a cry for the liberation from suffering of the living, a shout of indignation at the bestiality of war. In a programme note Cohan called *Mass* 'a re-working of the idea of X, which I choreographed after hearing the news of the My Lai massacres.' His dances insisted upon the torment and vain supplications of the victims of battle.

Immediately after this regional tour the company took off on their longest and most arduous foreign trip to date. They were to visit South America, appearing in Brazil, Argentina, Peru, Chile, Colombia, Venezuela and Mexico.*

*The company was unable to make a scheduled visit to El Salvador. The doors of the plane were too small to take the scenery, and the company returned to Rio to give an extra, free performance for Labour Day. An audience of workers proved, in Cohan's words 'the best we ever had'.

The tour was hard, enthusiastically received, and not without incidents, as the company battled with all the variations of climate, of theatre and of living accommodation. Technical problems loomed concerning the adaptation of the repertory (which included *Cell*, *Dance Energies*, *Cold*, *Cantabile*, *Eclipse*, *People Alone* and *People Together*) to a wide variety of theatres. In Buenos Aires, the day's class and rehearsals were separated by a lengthy break when the resident opera company required the stage for their own rehearsals. For Janet Eager as administrator of the tour there came additional crisis when Jenny Henry, the wardrobe mistress, developed sudden appendicitis. 'Mop' Eager – as she has always been known to everyone at The Place, the nickname a survival of her schooldays – at once had to take over wardrobe duties as well as coping with the infinity of tasks in her own work. The drying of costumes in a humid climate taxed her ingenuity until she contrived to bribe one theatre's handyman to let costumes dry in a boiler-room. That the handyman then decamped for a siesta, leaving the costumes locked away, produced another tense moment – solved half an hour before curtain-up by the greasing of a palm that had a key to the boiler-room.

The tour was a tremendous success and the repertory variously touched symphathetic chords in certain countries. Talking about *Cell*, which showed six people trying to escape from a prison, Robert Cohan admitted that 'the prison could be self-made or even imaginary. The problem is left open. People come to me and say "Hey, you know about my problem", and I don't. *Cell* concerns everybody's problems. It is a catharsis for people. We performed it in Chile on this tour and the audience saw it as a statement about their political situation and it got a thirty minute ovation.'

Rested after the tour, the company returned to The Place on 22 August for a season that brought the London showing of *Mass* and the first performance of an admirably contrasting work, Richard Alston's *Lay-Out*. As opposed to the searing emotions of Cohan's work, Alston offered an ordered arrangement of dances and a very cool precision of outline. The work developed from *Combines*, staged the previous year, and the movement offered a series of variations upon basic ideas expanded into an airy structure of solos and group dances. It was a piece of almost transparent clarity and remarkable purity of style.

There followed another short regional sortie with *Stages* and the full company's first tour of Scotland with *Stages* and a repertory programme. Robert Cohan was interviewed in the *Scotsman* by Una Flett, and in the course of the conversation he observed that a mere six years after his arrival, contemporary dance had clearly become part of the fabric of the nation's artistic life. 'When I first came (in 1967) there were enough students to make up one class. Now I am auditioning three or four hundred people for about sixty places at the School.'

The revival of *Stages* for this tour was a prelude to LCDT's boldest move yet in London: a week's season at Sadler's Wells from 30 October–3 November.

In his by now customary programme note Robin Howard was happy to be able 'to present the Dance Theatre's work to a larger London audience in a large London theatre.' Prophetically he added 'if this week is a success, we hope to return many more times.'

The gamble of a Wells season paid off handsomely. Robert North was dashingly the hero on the first night and the audience, as the *Financial Times* noted, was very young and 'like an Osmond overflow in enthusiasm'.

James Monahan summed up the advantages of the Wells season as an audience-building exercise, writing in the *Guardian* that the company

> has ventured for this week from its sanctuary at The Place, where there is room only for the faithful, to Sadler's Wells where the potential audience is larger and more heterogeneous. A milestone in the young life of this most modernist of our modern dance organisations, it has taken only one sample with it to the Wells, Robert Cohan's proven success, the full length *Stages*; and a wise choice too. Not because this 'impression in two parts of a Heromyth' (so it describes itself) is the best or most serious or most typical offering in the Dance Theatre's repertory. In my view, it is none of those things. But, what with its lavish use of gimmickry, its elaborate three tiered setting and the loud and mostly cheerful accompaniment of Bob Downes's Open Music, it makes a show which could be enjoyed by people who would be bored or frightened by the obscurities and austerities of much modern dance.

The year, though, was to end in tragedy. The Company had already suffered the loss of Frederick Bromwich, senior director of the Trust, who had died in March after devoted service to dance (he had for many years helped shape the destiny of Ballet Rambert). Now, during a performance of *Stages* at the Opera House, Manchester, at the beginning of December, Celeste Dandeker had fallen and cracked a vertebra in her neck during one of the acrobatic feats that come towards the end of the work. She was carried off stage by one of the male dancers and rushed to hospital, where it soon emerged that she was to be almost completely paralysed. At the age of twenty-two, the dance career of this gifted and beautiful young woman was brought to an end. With remarkable courage Celeste Dandeker has done much since that terrible time to help herself and to give expression to her other artistic abilities. She has designed for a number of companies, and also writes poetry.

1974

◆

In the early touring months of 1974, LCDT staged two new works at the Nuffield Theatre, Southampton: Siobhan Davies' *Pilot* and Robert North's *Dressed to Kill* – his fourth piece to enter the repertory. *Pilot* was assured, economical in showing a group of travellers passing the time in what seemed to be stop-overs in some interminable series of flights – it could well have been been a reflection of the previous year's South American journeyings. A Jew's harp and a harmonica played on stage provided the accompaniment, and the group of passengers occasionally clustered round an oil lamp in the gloom. It was a short work, very atmospheric and utterly secure in style and structure, and it included a beautiful solo for Linda Gibbs and an irresistible blues for the choreographer and Robert North. *Dressed to Kill* was a joking homage to the world of Raymond Chandler. North himself was the Philip Marlow figure, with the cast variously disguised as Marty the Mouth (Patrick Harding-Irmer, already attracting notice in his first year with the Company), Ever-Open Alice (Kate Harrison) and so on, characters who seemed to have strayed in from a Damon Runyon story. The piece was somewhat wittier in its design, by Peter Farmer, than in its dances, though it did boast a real red herring among its properties.

Both these novelties were seen at the Shaw Theatre when LCDT joined in the Camden 74 Festival from 26 February to 2 March. The Shaw Theatre, as the *Financial Times* noted, enhanced dancers and choreography: 'The stage, deeper and wider than at The Place, gives space and air round the bodies.' The programme began with Alston's *Lay-Out*, now re-titled *Blue Schubert Fragments* and set to different music, and continued with the first London appearance of Anna Sokolow's *Steps of Silence*, a characteristically anxious study, its cast looking like the last sad relics of a camp for displaced persons. Their mouthings of grief and pain had static power, but there was little interest in the dynamics of the piece and, inevitably, the cast had to produce 'the Sokolow stare', glowering meaningfully at the audience. The score, by the contemporary Romanian composer Anatole Vieru, was grindingly unattractive and the cast had a dreadful time, ending up naked and derelict amid a litter of old newspapers. As a music royalty of £250 per performance was demanded, it is not surprising that the piece soon slipped from the repertory.

Another imported choreography was very different: Remy Charlip's *Mad River*, with chic designs by the couturier Bill Gibb, was a re-working of five earlier dances. By turns grave and gay, they were attractively set on their cast

Linda Gibbs, Ross McKim, Siobhan Davies, Robert North and Patrick Harding-Irmer in Siobhan Davies's Pilot *(1974)*

and, as John Percival commented in *Dance and Dancers*, were clearly 'the work of an amateur in the best sense – someone who does a thing because he loves it'.

This was also a time of development for the School, which now had 120 full-time and 200 part-time students and could report that thirty local education authorities assisted with their grants. A fund-raising gala at The Place on 28 March brought the appearance of student dancers in Anna Sokolow's *Ballade*, to music by Scriabin, and *Three Poems*, along with the first performance by LCDT of Martha Graham's *Diversion of Angels*. The health of the school was further in evidence in October when the Gulbenkian Foundation announced a new grant of £20,500 over a period of three years. This would help towards the establishing of a Department of Choreography, to be directed by Nina Fonaroff, and it is not without significance that in May the West Midlands Arts

Association also announced that it would fund a scholarship worth £1,000 to the School.

For the Trust itself the year brought a new chairman, the property tycoon Gabriel Harrison. His appearance had been sudden. As Robin Howard recounts:

> We were considering the purchase of the freehold of The Place, since the owners of the building were talking of developing the site within a few years unless we could raise funds to purchase. In an attempt to play for time, I had the front façade on Duke's Road scheduled as of historic value and I was searching for money so as to be able to buy the building. One morning I had a telephone call from Lord Gibson, then Chairman of the Arts Council, regretting that the Council could not give us as much as they, or we, would have liked and saying that even at the moment of this phone call he had a possible benefactor in his office. This proved to be Gabriel Harrison and as he spoke for this first time he announced that he was prepared to give some generous funding: a promise of £250,000 and, if he liked what we were doing, a further £250,000 to follow. After we had met and the Board had been told of this generosity, it was agreed that he should assume Chairmanship of the Trust, and that we should start negotiating to take over The Place. Our immediate problems about a home seemed solved.

In the meantime, the life of the company and school went on, and in May a second European tour was undertaken – a six-week visit, with a repertory of eleven works, to theatres in Belgium, France, Switzerland and Germany. The British Council offered partial support, and after opening the tour in Belgium, the company arrived in Paris at the Théâtre de la Ville, home of Parisian experimental dance, for a sold-out and very well received season of *Stages* and a quadruple bill. Thence the company moved to the Lausanne International Festival and the creation at the Théâtre de Beaulieu of the specially-commissioned *Waterless Method of Swimming Instruction* by Robert Cohan. This was a *capriccio* set in a dry pool on board an ocean liner. Wittily set and costumed by Ian Murray Clark, it had its cast disporting themselves as if inspired by the manual which gave the piece its title. As counterpoint to the dance activity there was Siobhan Davies as the Siren of the Deck Chair, an irresistible piece of clowning, worthy of Bea Lillie, which found Davies as a gauche girl to whom the putting up of a deck chair and dressing and undressing herself for sunbathing assumed the proportions of World War III.

When the company moved on to Germany, circumstances and football were against them. 'We were' recalls Jane Eager, 'Julian Braunsweg's last scandal.* He had booked us to tour Germany at the time of the World Cup. There was hardly anybody in the theatre to watch *Stages*, and the stage manager would call out instructions to his staff and find no-one to carry them out as the men

---

*Braunsweg, an impresario, had called his memoirs *Braunsweg's Ballet Scandals*.

Patrick Harding-Irmer with members of the London Contemporary Dance Theatre in Anna Sokolow's Steps of Silence *(1974)*

were all watching the World Cup on television. We played a sports hall in Dusseldorf, and it was there that Dr Braunsweg announced that funds had run out and he could no longer pay us. The alternatives were to press on with the tour, with only our hotel bills paid, or to return home at once. Despite the poor houses owed to the World Cup, we had to continue. Dr Braunsweg disappeared to sell some jewels in order to pay our daily allowance, and thus we got through what was to be our only bad tour.'

More creations marked the company's return to touring in Britain, and a season at the Royal Northern College of Music in Manchester saw the first performance of Siobhan Davies's new piece, *The Calm*. Cool, lucid in form and texture, this was a work with a fine score by Geoffrey Burgon for counter-tenor, trumpet, violin and harp, which contrasted contemplative choreography for the choreographer and Namron with the quietly joyful work of five other dancers. It revealed, above everything else, the steadily developing gifts of its creator, and was much admired.

The other new piece was an acquisition from Dan Wagoner (whose company had appeared at The Place the previous year), *Changing Your Mind*. This curiosity began with a quartet for three girls and a man set to readings, by Ross McKim, of numbers and haphazard short news stories from a daily paper. There followed, though, another news story, clearly pre-ordained, concerning a Cherokee brave and his wife who killed themselves rather than live in poverty. Their story was told as a duet for Patrick Harding-Irmer and Cathy Lewis; both of them very touching.

When the tour reached Liverpool, a new work had joined the repertory, Robert North's *Spartan* (later *Troy*) *Games* – a display of muscular humour and bravura dancing which had been inspired in part by the rhythms of batucada music heard during the previous year's South American tour. By the time the company reached London for a three-week appearance at Sadler's Wells, North and Siobhan Davies had been nominated associate choreographers of the company and the season, successful as ever, brought the London showing of an exhilarating repertory that had been produced during the year.

Very properly the first programme at Sadler's Wells ended with *Diversion of Angels* which, said the *Financial Times*, announced for all the world to see that LCDT had come of age. 'Given with an exultant sense of joy and a lovely gaiety, this radiant work was radiantly danced; and to do it so well, so idiomatically, suggests the strength of training, and understanding, that only comes with maturity.' Robert Cohan's *Hunter of Angels* and *Eclipse* were revived, and William Louther returned as guest in Ailey's *Hermit Songs*, the grandeur and diversity of his dancing singularly beautiful. And as a final creation for the year, Cohan produced *No Man's Land*. This was an imaginative re-working of the Orpheus myth on Cocteau-esque terms, with a virtuoso score for double-bass played on stage by its composer, Barry Guy, and with Peter Farmer's brilliantly allusive design. A light bridge served as entry to the Underworld. Economical costuming

Paula Lansley in Remy Charlip's Mad River *(1974)*

OVERPAGE: Siobhan Davies (top centre) with members of the company in Robert Cohan's Waterless Method of Swimming Instruction *(1974)*

The men of London
Contemporary Dance Theatre
in Robert North's Troy Game
(1974)

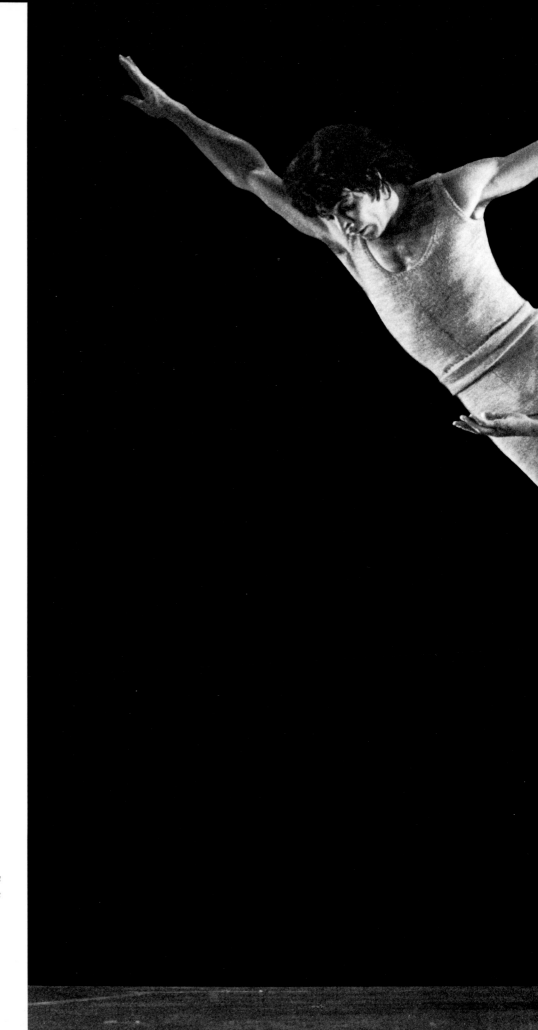

Linda Gibbs and Anthony van Laast in Siobhan Davies's The Calm *(1973)*

was in black and red for the denizens of the Underworld, white and beige for Orpheus and Eurydice, roles ideally taken by Robert North and Linda Gibbs. *No Man's Land* was visually, dynamically and emotionally one of the finest pieces yet created by LCDT.

The programme concluded with *Stages*, the hero's role shared by Micha Bergese and Robert North. With six London premieres and the company on its very best form, Robin Howard and Robert Cohan could feel justifiably proud at the end of this season. With the news that the autumn term at the School had 330 students, with Gulbenkian support for the new choreographic studies, and with Gabriel Harrison as benefactor and Chairman to secure the future of The Place itself, there was good reason to believe that some dreams had already been fulfilled and there were no regrets at the final collapse of the plan to move to Hammersmith in the late autumn, which would have demanded a commitment of £1 million from the Trust.

Alas, at the year's end there came the news of the sudden death of Gabriel Harrison. He had entered hospital for a minor operation and had died quite unexpectedly. He also died intestate, and without making any of the benefactions that had been anticipated to secure The Place finally and permanently for The Trust. The Trust already had a moral obligation to purchase the freehold in Duke's Road and Harrison had promised massive funds at Board meetings and intended to lead an Appeals Committee for the future of the entire enterprise. Thus by the spring of 1975 Robin Howard and the Trust were faced with their worst crisis so far. The half a million pounds anticipated from Gabriel Harrison was lost; a further £30,000 had been spent on work and plans for the future. There seemed no possibility that these sums could be covered.

Siobhan Davies and Robert North in Robert Cohan's No Man's Land *(1974)*

1975

◆

While the grave problems connected with the Trust's financial future loomed, the life of the company continued with its customary vigour. It made its usual appearance at the Camden Festival (which 'has livened up that most deadly of months, February', noted Peter Williams) between 18 February and 1 March at the Shaw Theatre. Four premieres marked the season, with Robert North's *Still Life* shown first on 18 February. This was an exercise in the use of film as an adjunct and extension of dance, in a story of a young man liberating himself from his family and embarking on a love affair, moving between live performance and filmed sequences. It was well staged, and well designed by Peter Farmer, but less well worked out in resolving all the narrative problems of its new style. Two days later Micha Bergese's *Hinterland* showed an apprentice talent making its mark with a study of three women who recall an early love for the same man, while on the same programme Robert Cohan's *Myth* was a somewhat hermetic though vigorously danced commentary upon heroic attitudes between men and women. The final new work was *Extinction*, a revision of an earlier surreal workshop piece by Cathy Lewis. Like the other creations for the season it could hardly be accounted a success.

As part of the Camden festivities, and as a valuable exercise in audience-building, the company offered groups 'the chance to find out more about modern dance'. An enterprising series of options included the opportunity to watch choreographers at work, to sample a class, and for teenage boys, a chance to watch *Troy Game* in performance. There were free posters, lecture demonstrations and classes at reduced prices, and a visit to the School.

The by now annual event of a gala for student funds took place in June when Lynn Seymour, a ballerina of the Royal Ballet, appeared as guest artist dancing a duet with Robert North: *Poem*, set to Scriabin music, had choreography by Bernd Berg. The gala also brought the first performance of a then untitled but exhilarating display of Graham technique by Robert Cohan, which would soon be admired under the title *Class* (its public premiere came in Aberdeen in September during the company's autumn tour). As a complementary exercise a film was shown, *This is The Place*, which was concerned with the many activities of the Trust, and ran for forty minutes. Its showing launched an appeal for an Endowment Fund of £1.1 million and in October the Earl of Drogheda, President of the Trust, made a statement concerning the plans for the Trust's future:

The Place is the centre for contemporary dance in Europe. But even, and perhaps especially, in these inflationary and austere times, the very nature of the organisation demands that we find means to develop and expand. The energy and creativity is already there; so is the reputation and the brilliance. What we do need desperately is more space. The lease on the present building at 17 Duke's Road can be terminated during 1976. We now have the opportunity to buy the freehold of The Place and that of an adjoining property. We need £650,000 to purchase these freeholds, £200,000 for conversion and improvements and £250,000 for a development fund to finance activities for which Contemporary Dance Trust can not obtain official monetary grants.

And so, undaunted by the financial tribulations of the year, LCDT took up residence in Rosebery Avenue for the Sadler's Wells season from 12 November

Kate Harrison with the women of London Contemporary Dance Theatre in Robert Cohan's Stabat Mater *(1975)*

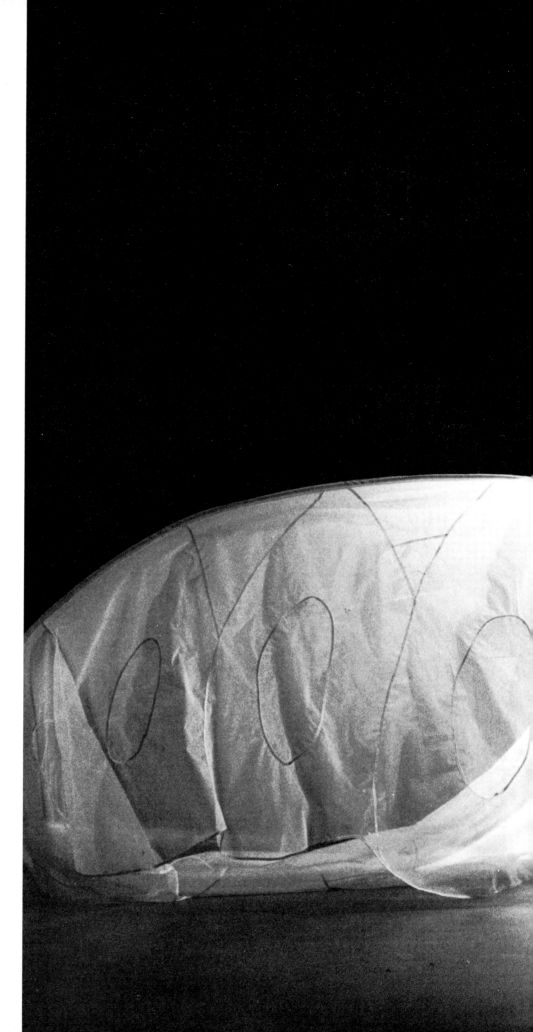

Paula Lansley in Robert Cohan's Masque of Separation *(1975)*

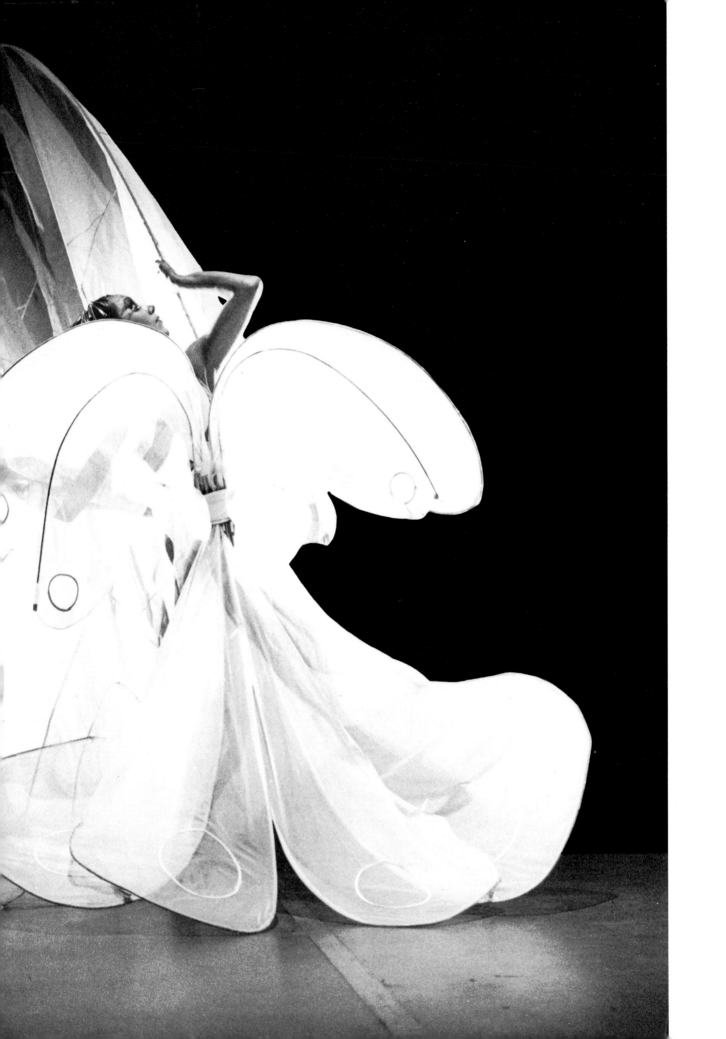

to 13 December. There was a repertory of seventeen works, of which seven were new to London, and despite the fact that a couple of leading dancers were unavailable to perform because of injury, attendance was eager. In his introduction to the programme Robin Howard reiterated points already made by Lord Drogheda concerning funds:

> So, we decided to fight our way out of financial trouble, by starting a fund-raising campaign and by trying to earn extra income, rather than by making any further cuts which would, inevitably, have affected our standards. This is the main reason why, this year, we have taken on the challenge of a five week season. It is unheard of for a contemporary dance company to perform for that long in one large theatre but, as we reached an audience capacity of over 80% during our one week here in 1973, and again during three weeks in 1974 and, as we could offer such diverse and exciting programmes, we decided to take the risk.

Programming began, very properly, with a Cohan evening. *Class* was recognised by public and critics as an exultant display of Graham technique, as Cohan had implanted it in Britain, and of the company's superb technical standards. *Stabat Mater*, which had received its first performance in Scotland during the autumn tour, brought the touching beauty of Kate Harrison's performance as the central point of this delicate work which used Vivaldi's setting of the verse. Like many of Graham's own works, Cohan's piece used an attendant chorus to display facets of the Virgin Mary's emotions. (A decade later it was to be seen in the marvellous setting of Canterbury Cathedral when church and university joined dancers of LCDT in celebration of the granting of the first degrees in dance by the University of Kent.) This first evening closed with *Masque of Separation*, which was *Myth* re-titled though no more easily comprehensible than under its old name, albeit performance and choreography aroused admiration.

The acquisition of *Headlong* from Richard Alston's Strider acknowledged the significance of Alston's individual and clean-lined choreography, which fixed images of falling and flight on the bodies of Siobhan Davies, Linda Gibbs, Anthony van Laast, and Ross McKim. Micha Bergese's *Da Capo al fine*, a product of his participation in the first Gulbenkian Summer School that year, was an experiment in analysing personal experience which was not entirely successful. William Louther returned again as a breathtaking guest artist in his own *Vesalii Icones*. Two collaborative works by Robert North, in which he also danced, were on view. The first, *Gladly, Badly, Sadly, Madly*, was a duet about ways of love created with and for Lynn Seymour, which both artists danced with wonderful commitment; the second was *David and Goliath*, made with Wayne Sleep of the Royal Ballet, in which the two performers saw their roles in terms of their own contrasted physiques, but also looked below the surface of the Biblical story to suggest that North's Goliath was a giant wearied of war, while Sleep's David was a bellicose and militaristic figure. Very different was

Wayne Sleep and Robert North in David and Goliath, *which they choreographed jointly in 1975*

Anca Frankenhaeuser in Robert Cohan's Place of Change *(1975)*

the world of Siobhan Davies's *Diary*, which comprised succinct and elegant entries from the physical memories she retained of work in the late spring, with the resultant dance clear and fresh in atmosphere. And equally different from this was Robert Cohan's *Place of Change*, receiving its London showing: an emotionally tense realisation of Schoenberg's Second String Quartet which he had made for the Bat-Dor company in Israel during the summer, it was concerned with the transmutation of earthly love into spiritual feeling.

For Cohan the year ended with an accolade not just reflecting the present excellence of his company but also recognising what he had achieved during the preceding eight years. The London *Evening Standard* offered annual awards for theatre, ballet and opera, and for 1975 the ballet panel unanimously decided that Cohan's was the 'outstanding achievement' which would merit this most prestigious prize. Cohan might also have been awarded a prize for economics. In *Time Out* Jan Murray, writing about the financial crisis that haunted LCDT, cited the fact that 'All of the 18 new works mounted by LCDT this past year have been staged on a total budget of £15,000. Compare this sum with the £70,000 reportedly lashed out by the Royal Ballet to refurbish a perfectly acceptable production of *Romeo and Juliet*, and with the £150,000 spent on Festival Ballet's new *Sleeping Beauty*.'

Lynn Seymour and Robert North in Gladly, Badly, Sadly, Madly *(1975)*

Cathy Lewis and Anthony van Laast in Siobhan Davies's Diary *(1975)*

1976

◆

Accolades also awaited Robin Howard in the New Year; the Honours List saw him awarded the CBE, while the Royal Academy of Dancing presented him with its Queen Elizabeth II Coronation Award for 'Outstanding Service to the Art of Ballet'. The continued expansion of the Trust's activities and, implicitly, the wisdom of its policies was borne out by the first of a series of 'residencies'. These were suggested by Howard and initiated by Cohan, in emulation of the American modern dance tradition whereby a dance company took up residence in a college or centre of education and worked there, teaching, creating, involving students and members of a local community in the activities of the troupe. The first LCDT residencies in Yorkshire and Humberside were sponsored between January and March by the Arts Associations of Yorkshire, Lincolnshire and Humberside. They found LCDT split in half; one group of nine dancers, a choreographer, a musician and two technicians at work, while other members of the company took sabbatical leave or worked in London. In later years the second half of the company also fulfilled concurrent residencies in other parts of the country. In this first experimental session the company appeared at Bradford and Bingley College, Hull University, York University, Lady Mabel College near Sheffield, Bretton Hall near Wakefield, Aberystwith for a week of perfomances, a week of performances and a residency in Nottingham, and finally three weeks at the I. M. Marsh College of Physical Education near Liverpool. As Cohan told *Dance and Dancers*, 'I was looking for an alternative way for the company to function. You see, our normal way of functioning now is to do between 20 and 25 weeks of straight performing a year. It's very hard and it's, in a sense, uncreative in that the dancers never get to meet the audience or know what the audience is thinking about what they are doing. We have always tried to do lecture demonstrations along the way, one afternoon a week, then we would also teach some master classes. It seemed to me that this could be expanded. At the time, several members of the company, who have been with us for a long time, wanted some time off to do some work.'

The success of this enterprise was never in doubt. The long residency at I. M. Marsh College helped, as the College put it, 'to share work with teachers, students and children – to look at the problems of dance in schools and colleges through specific examples and to offer help and constructive comment.' And at the same time Cohan was fulfilling one of the necessary activities of a residency: he was creating a new dance work, *Khamsin*. As Rosemary Hartill

Anca Frankenhaeuser and Namron in Khamsin *(1976)*

wrote in the *Times Educational Supplement* about the concept of residency: 'Perhaps the most demanding sessions have been the open rehearsals, where new works are created and rehearsed. Over five days at Bretton Hall in Yorkshire, ten successive groups of 150 spectators at a time watched the company create a new dance called *Khamsin* which is to be premiered in Leeds on March 22 . . . Robert Cohan says that the only difference between the Bretton Hall and normal choreographic sessions was that the tape was at a more advanced stage than usual and the pauses when he thought what he was going to do next had to be rather shorter.'

The Yorkshire residency bore exceptional fruit. As a first means of finding a new audience, Cohan sent the men of the company round schools in the area to rehearse and perform *Troy Game* in gymnasia and sports centres. He then announced that if there were more men than women in the paying open classes, there would be no charge for the class. The canny students understood what this meant and most of the girls brought their boy friends. Classes became free and, more important, there were thirty applicants for the School at the end of the residency. Of these, twenty-two were accepted into the School and no fewer than seventeen graduated over three years later.

It was at this time that Cohan went to London to receive the *Evening Standard* Award, which was presented to him at the Savoy Hotel on 4 February by Lynn Seymour. In his speech of acceptance Cohan declared that the award was really for Robin Howard and the whole of the LCDT organisation: 'Robin has given all his money to us, but it has made him very happy. Now,' glancing round the crowded dining-room with a gentle smile 'if any of you would like to be very happy. . .'

Howard's happiness may be judged from the fact that on 1 March at Sotheby's his collection of Elizabethan and Jacobean books, ranging from Shakespeare folios to cookery books, was sold for £184,000. The funds, inevitably, were to be used for the Trust.

With the residencies over, the company returned to London for the now traditional Camden Festival season, between 16 and 20 March, and the programmes at The Place reflected the educational nature of the residencies experiment. James Monahan in the *Guardian* discussed the programming, which featured explanation about the repertory as part of the entertainment: 'I have been to two of their explanatory programmes this week at The Place, the one devoted mainly to a work by Cohan called *Class*, the other to North's *Troy Game*. *Class* is a trimmed and only slightly glamourised account of the company's daily training and calls for relatively little explanation. Still, it comes across all the better when the audience can concentrate wholly on its wealth of movement and grouping and does not go needlessly hunting for a hidden message.' The *Financial Times* observed that Robert Cohan could declare 'we now do everything in public'. The paper also noted that the recent residencies had, each week, brought three days of open classes and lecture demonstrations followed by three days in the

Linda Gibbs and Robert North in Robert Cohan's Nymphéas *(1976)*

OVERPAGE: Nymphéas

nearest theatre with performances which included a matinee 'open forum' costing the viewer a princely 10p. Each night during this Camden season a work was analysed. Cohan dissected *Cell* on one occasion and the *Financial Times* commented that Cohan's analysis yet managed to keep *Cell's* focus and interest. He talked the audience through a performance without score and with dancers in practice dress, and then with all the themes and incidents thus exposed, could put the ballet together again most illuminatingly for his public in theatrical performance.

The one novelty of the Festival was the first London showing of Namron's *The Bronze*, a light-hearted piece about the statue of an athlete which comes to life and is finally toppled from its pedestal when a child throws a ball at it.

From Camden the company set off on tour to Leeds where, on 22 March, the first performance was given of *Khamsin*, on which Cohan had been so publicly working. Concerned with the desert wind of the Sahara that can derange the passions, it was emotionally charged and visually powerful in its use of fabric, which became part of the choreographic action. In York, as part of the Festival, Cohan also created *Nymphéas* with funds provided by the Arts Council. Inspired by Monet's late paintings of water lilies, this Impressionist work found its cast clad in tights dappled in Monet's colours. A white set by Norberto Chiesa allowed the dance to ripple and eddy against it, while Debussy piano music provided a sympathetic accompaniment.

The summer brought a remarkable commentary upon the changed nature of dance appreciation in Britain. As part of the US bicentennial celebrations, Martha Graham's company appeared at the Royal Opera House, Covent Garden, storming this bastion of classic ballet in grand style. The success of the Graham season reflected the new climate of feeling in Britain about contemporary dance, which was the fruit of Howard's and Cohan's work during the thirteen years since Graham had last appeared in London.

Meantime, LCDT was invited in late July to the Santander Festival, and in October was again in Europe. A couple of performances at the Styrian Autumn Festival of New Dance at Graz on 9 and 10 October brought the first performance of Micha Bergese's *Nema*. Identified as the Greek for 'the thread of a man's life', *Nema* dealt rather earnestly with the shadows cast by the past. With British Council support the company had also appeared in Belgium at the beginning of October at the Hainault International Festival, in Spain at the Zarzuela Theatre in Madrid, and in Portugal, appearing under the auspices of the Gulbenkian Foundation in its auditorium in Lisbon.

At this same time the Trust was finally able to purchase the freehold of The Place, with some of Robin Howard's funding coming from the sale of his books and a further £180,000 produced by the sale of land which he owned jointly with his brother. Discussing this important moment in the Trust's life, Howard reflected that up to this time he had been regarded 'as the rich man who pottered

with the arts and gave of his surplus. Then I had to decide whether really to
do something. So with my brother I agreed to sell our farm. I had sold my book
collection and got rid of all my shares. And I've been beautifully clean ever since.
For The Place we received £100,000 from Arts Council funding for Housing
the Arts; the Linbury Trust was very generous in giving us £50,000. There were
a few other small donations though none of any great size, though the GLC
offered something. I had ultimately to provide about £600,000 of which half
was to be a long term loan.'

The company returned to England for an autumn tour of the regions and
it is evidence of their increased popularity that in both 1975 and 1976 LCDT
could play the Royal Northern College of Music in Manchester to 98% capacity
audiences. It was Manchester that saw the first perfomance of Siobhan Davies's
new *Step at a Time*, a work of 'white' choreography that carefully argued the
merits of movement purged of any emotional clutter. The dance stressed line
and the emergence of precise forms from imprecision, and it could be seen as
commenting implicitly on the creative act itself in refining stylised movement
from the swirl of everyday activity.

By late November LCDT was back at Sadler's Wells for a three-week season
from 30 November to 18 December. In his now usual summing-up of the state
of play for his audience – whom he considered, very rightly, as part of his LCDT
family – Robin Howard wrote: 'In the last year the London Contemporary
Dance Theatre has worked incredibly hard, producing nine new ballets and performing for over 32 weeks; our dancers have appeared nearly every night and
most have been taking solo parts. As 26 of these weeks have been touring this
is more than we can do every year.'

Fourteen works by six choreographers comprised the repertory and the new
works for the London season included *Khamsin* and *Nymphéas*, *Step at a Time*,
Nema and Robert North's spoof *Just a Moment*. In this piece, six dancers came
on stage calling out their names, and were thereafter caught up in encounters
sometimes happy, sometimes more serious. There were coloured projections to
show off the dances and the overall effect was unpretentious and light-hearted.

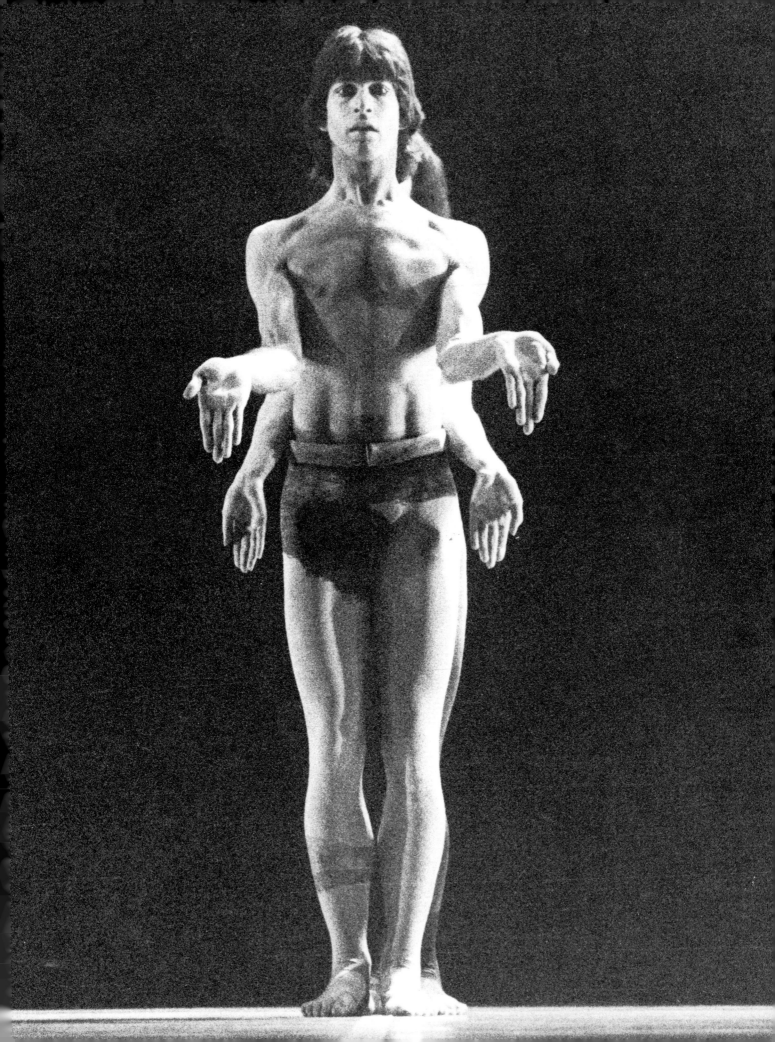

1977

◆

Nineteen seventy-seven began with LCDT in residence in Yorkshire again, and in Lancaster. The Yorkshire residency at Bretton Hall was the subject of a television documentary by Derek Bailey for his London Weekend Television arts programme *Aquarius*, and in the *Financial Times* Clement Crisp provided immediate reportage of events: in diary form he charted three days of company activity:

Wednesday. The *Aquarius* team under producer Derek Bailey, who is also to direct this programme, arrives to find LCDT settled in and working hard. Robert Cohan and nine of his dancers are staying at Bretton; the rest of the company is spending the fortnight in residence at Padgate and at Lancaster University. Each day begins with class given for the Bretton students, while other members of the company go to teach class in local schools. After lunch, and company class, the afternoon comprises two 90-minute sessions in which Cohan and Micha Bergese are creating (in full view of an audience) two sections of *Successions*. This is the working title for a celebratory piece, commisioned for the Silver Jubilee season at the Wells in April, which is to be made by all four LCDT's resident choreographers. Robert North and Siobhan Davies – who are at Padgate – are working on their sections while Bergese and Cohan create at Bretton, with Bob Downes, the composer, in attendance. The immediacy of this creativity, the insights offered the audience about the physical and psychological labours of making a work of art, are uniquely fascinating. Furthermore, ballets due to be seen at Harrogate next week are also being rehearsed. Among them, Bergese's *Nema* and Cohan's *Khamsin* (which was actually created at Bretton last year).

In the evening, after a break, there follows a master class for Bretton students and any other teachers and students who have enrolled. The winter chill is a problem, but heaters blaze determinedly, and the LCDT dancers – who are 'on view' throughout their very long day – move in and out of layers of wool as temperature and work dictate.

Thursday. The morning school visit is to the magnificent new Featherstone High School. Class is held in an imaginative open-plan drama area, and Anthony van Laast works with about 30 girls, with a new member of LCDT, Philippe Giraudeau, as demonstrator (the usual system with teaching sessions). The girls come from three local schools, and van Laast's instruction

Anthony van Laast in Robert Cohan's Forest *(1977)*

is sympathetic, stressing the absolute essentials of good posture, and correct placing of the body in the simplest of exercises.

Robert Cohan moves among the pupils to give slight corrections, and after 45 minutes he and van Laast exchange roles. By the end of the class the girls leave looking very proud and moving just that fraction better. Cohan and van Laast have spoken to them with great perception about dancing. (Martha Graham's dictum about the need for sending the very best dancers to teach children, is resolutely maintained by LCDT – and should be remembered by everyone connected with dance for the young.)

Back at Bretton, company class is taken after lunch by Linda Gibbs, and the bodies of the dancers as they stretch and leap are intensely pleasing: dancers are never truer to themselves or more beautiful than in class. An audience of teachers and children now arrive with news of snow falling as the afternoon rehearsal session begins. Micha Bergese works on a lyrical section for four girls, in *Successions*, and then rehearses *Nema*. By 4.30 in the afternoon when Cohan starts his rehearsal, the news is that a blizzard has started, but Cohan is more concerned with his next section of *Successions* because he has used up all the music that Bob Downes has completed for him. Consultations between them follow, with Downes taking notes and working on the score, while Cohan explains the dance in progress to a newly arrived audience. The sense of dedicated work, the communion between the dancers and their choreographers, is very exciting, and the TV crew move delicately and sometimes almost invisibly among them.

By the time of the evening session, the blizzard has set in. Roads are impassable, but there is class still for the Bretton students.

Friday. Although the countryside now looks like a set for *Nanook of the North*, Micha Bergese and Paula Lansley are with Robert Cohan and the TV crew at a school some 20 miles from Bretton by 10.30. The pattern of the day is the same as Thursday. Bergese gives a stimulating class, with Lansley and Cohan demonstrating and correcting: the pleasure is in seeing how they set about sculpting a better physical stance from the young bodies they are working with. Company class back at Bretton reminds one of the grand results of the dancers' daily sweated labour, as Linda Gibbs flashes through the air, and Patrick Harding-Irmer rides easily on top of a huge jump.

The other dancers, van Laast, Bergese, Lansley, Cathy Lewis, Charlotte Milner, Anca Frankenhäuser and Giraudeau, look equally splendid and they are untiringly responsive to Cohan as he teaches and later rehearses *Khamsin* for an audience. Watching Cohan at work I am vividly reminded of his extraordinary qualities as a dancer with Graham – he is still, effortlessly, a unique exponent of the Graham style at its most powerful. He is also, as teacher and speaker, a charismatic figure and his exposition of the themes and imagery of *Khamsin* is gripping as he explains how varied strands of experience have fed his choreographic text.

Siobhan Davies in Jane Dudley's Harmonica Breakdown *(1977)*

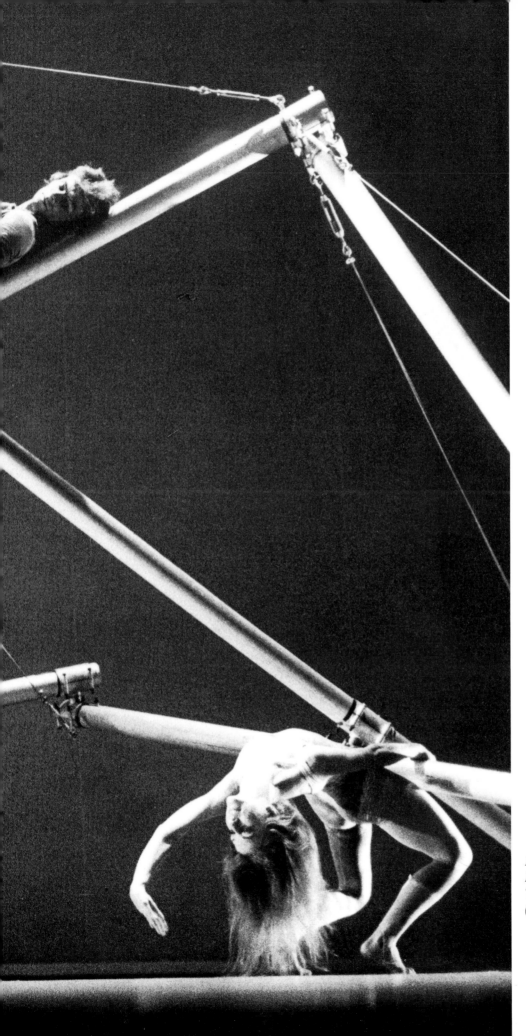

Micha Bergese with members of
London Contemporary Dance
Theatre in his own Continuum
(1977)

Saturday. Cohan and all the LCDT dancers travel to yet another country house turned training college for a double session – three hours – with a movement study group of teachers and students. Cohan gives class; his dancers demonstrate and correct – but as Cohan tells the class: 'You should correct yourselves. You are using me as your own conscience, and you *mustn't*. I'm not here too often, and you know what needs correcting.' But the need for LCDT's stimulus is very obvious, as too is Cohan's insistence on the need to understand the technical and anatomical basis for even the simplest dance movement.

Sunday will be a rest-day, and then on Monday the dancers will commute between Bretton, where they teach, and Harrogate where they perform and also give open rehearsals.

The developing of an audience through residencies was one bold initiative undertaken by LCDT; more traditional was the returning to regional theatres on an annual basis, and an analysis of touring and attendance at this time provides intriguing insights into the company's success in enlarging its public. Oxford and Cambridge had both been on the regular schedule of visits since 1973. Over a period of three years the audiences there had doubled, while the same excellent result was to be seen with Warwick and Manchester in the period from 1975 to 1977.

With the residencies finished, LCDT took to the road and presented its first creation of the year, Robert North's *Meeting and Parting*, in Oxford. The choreography studied a sequence of emotional incidents for four couples, where shifts in feeling were lightly examined to Howard Blake's attractive piano score. The success of the late autumn season at Sadler's Wells in recent years emboldened the company to consider a second London season in the year, and at Easter LCDT was again in Rosebery Avenue for three weeks, 5–23 April. They were also on television when, just before Easter itself, Thames Television presented a version of Vaughan Williams's *Job*. This was conceived for the small screen by Robert Cohan, with Robert North as Job, Siobhan Davies as Job's wife, Namron as Satan, and Ross McKim as Elihu. The production made use of television techniques to create visual effects impossible in the theatre, and the chorus played a remarkable collection of antique musical instruments.

At Sadler's Wells the company celebrated the Queen's Silver Jubilee with a new work which had been created during the residencies by four of the company's choreographers. With a commissioned score from Bob Downes and design by Norberto Chiesa, *Night Watch* was concerned with the passage of the hours of darkness. The programme offered no guidance as to who had created which section of the choreography, but the *Financial Times* opined that Cohan had produced the opening and linking sections, while Siobhan Davies was responsible for the lucid incident entitled 'Evening Star', with Micha Bergese responsible for a flowing 'Midnight Sun' section and Robert North the creator of 'Palais 4 a.m.', which showed young people dancing the night away.

Ironically this collaboration only seems to have encouraged its creators to be anonymous, and *Night Watch* was found to be too careful and too anaemic in style. Not so Robert Cohan's next creation for the season, *Forest*, where, against a soundtrack of wind and rain and the faint calls of birds and animals, the choreography beautifully explored images evoking the natural world and the habits of forest creatures. Exceptional among an exceptional cast, Anthony van Laast seemed the reincarnation of Nijinsky's faun in a new habitat, giving a performance which epitomised the sensitivity of this gifted work. In contrast there came Jane Dudley's revival of her own *Harmonica Breakdown*, a blues solo now re-staged for Siobhan Davies and admirably danced by her, even if she lacked something of the extraordinary power of Dudley's own dancing. Nearly forty years after its creation, *Harmonica Breakdown* offered a fascinating juxtaposition of strutting walks and sudden bursts of what looked like the Turkey Trot. At every performance, Siobhan Davies had a personal triumph.

Siobhan Davies in her own Sphinx (1977)

The Wells season was followed by a brief regional tour before the company's second appearance at the Théâtre de la Ville in Paris. For a three-week visit, with nine repertory works, the reception from public and critics was rapturous: Claude Baignières in *Le Figaro* wrote that 'the dancers of this young British troupe are infinitely gifted.' But greater things were ahead in the way of foreign reception. With what must have seemed extreme daring in taking coals to contemporary dance's Newcastle, LCDT accepted an invitation from the American Dance Festival at New London, Connecticut, proposing to travel onward from there to Wolf Trap, near Washington, the Temple Music Festival at Ambler, Philadelphia, and then on to Pennsylvania Park University.

On Thursday 30 June, the company made its US debut at the American Dance Festival with Siobhan Davies's *Diary 2* and Cohan's *Cell* and *Class*, following this the next night with Cohan's *Masque of Separation*, *Stabat Mater* and North's *Troy Game*. The reception from the local press was admirable – 'London Contemporary Dancers Make Smashing Debut in US' ran one headline – while Anna Kisselgoff in the *New York Times* wrote of 'a highly interesting, well trained company', and 'unquestionably deserved success'.

The first performance by London Contemporary Dance Theatre at New London was very special to Robert Cohan for many reasons, not least because he had danced there from the very beginning of the dance festival, notably in Graham's *Diversion of Angels*. More than usually nervous, he stood at the back of the auditorium watching the performance and as the evening ended with the exuberant energies of *Class*, there was a moment of silence and he saw the audience rise to their feet. His immediate reaction was 'My God! They're all leaving!' and it was not until the roar of applause broke out that he realised the company was being given a standing ovation. As he recounts, for days afterwards he was shaking with relief.

Robin Howard wrote in a press release: 'Ten years ago I invited Robert Cohan to London to start a contemporary dance company and an affiliated school. A decade later, LCDT made its debut at the American Dance Festival to a standing ovation. Press reports praised the discipline, conviction and rapport of our dancers, but the two most singularly valued comments underlying all the reviews were the recognition of our individual character and Cohan himself as an outstanding choreographer.'

The achievements of the US tour were considerable, not only in showing the American dance public that the imported Graham style had rooted and grown handsomely in Britain, but also in letting LCDT itself know that the company was now to be recognised as a major ensemble. Returning in triumph to Britain, the company embarked on its regional tour in the autumn, visiting Inverness where, on 30 September, a new work by Micha Bergese was premiered. *Continuum* was inspired by Albert Camus' *Myth of Sisyphus* and the stage was dominated by Norberto Chiesa's structure of angled aluminium masts which formed a series of slopes up which a mountaineer Sisyphus (Bergese himself)

Tom Jobe and Patrick Harding-Irmer in Richard Alston's Rainbow Bandit *(1977)*

for ever climbed and slid, while a group of dancers below provided commentary and contrast with this absurdist view of the hero.

Arriving in Manchester for a two-week season from 18–29 October at the Royal Northern College of Music, the company gave the first performance of Siobhan Davies's *Sphinx*, a delicate creation that again stressed the clarity and elegance of Davies's writing. The choreography concentrated on herself as the sphinx and five other dancers.

The undoubted success of regional tours such as these was set in perspective by the ever-present problems of financial security. The Place and its neighbouring building had been bought and were now being prepared for occupancy by company and school. In addition to the £400,000 already spent on the freehold, a further £350,000 was needed 'to complete extensions and alterations'. And Robin Howard observed in an appeal letter: 'We can meet some of this cost from our own resources, but a substantial sum remains to be raised. We have no doubt of the response from the public. British audiences for our own company have grown from 2,000 in 1967 to 80,000 in 1976, and are larger still in 1977 – to which must be added television audiences, as the company has done an average of one television show a year. Audiences abroad are now just under 40,000 a year.'

The early winter season at Sadler's Wells took place between 15 November and 10 December. It brought the London showings of *Sphinx* and *Continuum*, and the creation of a new piece by Richard Alston that marked his return to London after two years' work and study in New York with Merce Cunningham. *Rainbow Bandit*, performed to the ingratiating Charles Amirkhanian text of the words 'rainbow check bandit bomb', repeated canonically and ad infinitum, showed an increased assurance on the part of the choreographer and a clear sense in deploying bodies in space, with notably beautiful writing for Anca Frankenhaeuser and Patrick Harding-Irmer. In the middle of the season came a fund-raising gala for the building fund and the School, in which *Khamsin* and *Class* framed some divertissements. Lynn Seymour appeared as a lustrous guest in Lar Lubovitch's *Scriabin Dances*; Siobhan Davies repeated her *Harmonica Breakdown* success, and there were some fascinating Duncan reconstructions by Madeleine Lytton, who had studied with Lise Duncan. The girls of the company looked delightful in Duncan's two Schubert Waltzes and *Les Filles de Chalcis* (to an extract from Gluck's *Iphigénie*). The revival of one of Ted Shawn's all-male dances (the *Polonaise* for five men of the company) was risible. 'Loin-clothed beefcake, self-consciously virile and irresistibly funny,' said the *Financial Times*.

1978

◆

The year began with a third series of residencies. Results were as excellent as ever and creativity was maintained. As usual with the residencies, the company had been divided into two groups, and this division of forces was repeated during the spring, seven dancers appearing on a regional tour with Robert North, while seven others worked with Bergese. Only one problem troubled this arrangement when, during one week, injury to a dancer in one group meant that mid-week the groups had to exchange personnel and repertory so that the variety of performance could be maintained.

On 23 January in Harrogate Micha Bergese produced *When Summer's Breath*, a contemplation for three couples on three of Shakespeare's sonnets. There was an adventurous score by Michael Finnissy and the action was by turns lyric, impassioned and, in the final sonnet, almost ghostly. On this same programme Bergese also made for himself a solo, *Box*, in which he was subjected to all the indignities of the boxing ring. It was brief, but hardly compelling.

Robert North staged his Scriabin *Preludes and Studies* in Leicester on 23 February. The music ranged from the Chopinesque early preludes to some of the composer's late and visionary writing, and the dances took their emotional colour from this contrast. Five couples were involved with the action which centred upon an unhappy relationship between a man and two women.

Meanwhile a determined effort was made to raise more income from sponsorship by holding a reception and performance at the Mansion House, London, in April. The Anglo-American Contemporary Dance Foundation and the Anglo-American Exchange Committee, formed by Robin Howard to assist in the exchange of teachers and companies across the Atlantic, joined with the Trust in urging additional private and public support. The Lord Mayor of London, the Earl of Drogheda as Chairman of the Trust, and Robin Howard received many guests who were to see an exhibition of photographs by Anthony Crickmay – who had recorded LCDT's work from the very first, an exceptional tribute from one of the world's finest dance photographers – the duet from *Nymphéas*, performed by Linda Gibbs and Anthony van Laast, and Siobhan Davies in *Harmonica Breakdown*, as samples of the company's work.

On this occasion the work of the Trust was presented in very positive terms with some intriguing breakdown figures about audiences: 'In the regions some research (in 1975) shows that there is a very strong young bias in audience for the company's work: 57% of audiences are between 15 and 24, compared with

Anita Griffin and Tom Jobe in Micha Bergese's Solo Ride *(1978)*

17% of the total population, and only 6% aged over 45 compared with 44% of the population. Such a bias is not usual to all theatre or concert audiences and clearly reflects a particular attraction of the company.'

Plans for the future were set out clearly. They included a decision to develop the resources of The Place, and thus of the Trust, through a building programme; to extend the number and duration of scholarships; to develop community projects with dance and to foster exchanges between Britain and North America of teachers and performers.

After the excitements of the previous year's journeyings, the only foreign visit of the year was to Egypt, where the company gave performances in September in the Balloon Theatre in Cairo. Originally it had been intended that the company should dance at the Sphynx Theatre, located immediately in front of the pyramids and the sphynx itself, but this dramatic setting was to prove impossible when a pop group also appearing there was unable to effect a speedy get-out. Thus it was that the company transferred its performances to the enormous tent in the centre of Cairo known as the Balloon Theatre. The Cairene audience was enthusiastic. A visit to Alexandria was projected, but the management of the theatre there had optimistically supposed that LCDT would be able to start performing each evening immediately after a programme given by a circus. LCDT's visit had, regretfully, to be cancelled.

Class, *Forest* and *Troy Game* made up the Egyptian programme, and the only disadvantage of the Balloon Theatre was that its canvas walls let in traffic noise which sat rather at odds with the faint murmurings and soughing of the wind in *Forest's* soundtrack.

Returned for an autumn tour prior to the Sadler's Wells season, LCDT produced three more new works. Robert Cohan's *Eos* was concerned with the long watches of a sleepless night when the insomniac waits, a prey to every disquiet, for the faint changes of light that mark the coming of dawn. Siobhan Davies's *Then You Can Only Sing* was set to words and accompaniment by Judyth Knight, long time a favourite pianist with the company. It was a miscalculation on every count. Micha Bergese produced, in *Solo Ride*, what was thought to be his most mysterious and accomplished work to date. It teetered on the brink of surrealism as Tom Jobe appeared on stage riding a tricycle, a dummy *doppelganger* behind him, while four girls awaited his arrival. Jobe danced with each in turn, and though the choreography's meaning was not always clear, its vivid theatrical energy reflected the excellence of Jobe's dancing and the extraordinary vision that Bergese was seeking to communicate.

By the time the company reached Sadler's Wells for a season between 21 November and 16 December, there were seven works created during the year to be shown, together with a brand new piece by Cohan. This was *Ice* which, as he told *Classical Music Weekly*, was about 'the embodiment of that feeling we all have when we can't cope with something, your emotions freeze, your actions freeze, you become petrified with fear. I took that quality and personified it, and tried to make the statement that Ice-Death comes into a relationship

Anca Frankenhaeuser in Robert Cohan's Eos *(1978)*

and separates us, freezes us up.' Memorably performed, it brought Tom Jobe as a mysterious science-fiction figure haunting the relationship between Linda Gibbs and Patrick Harding-Irmer. Robert North also provided a second new piece for this season with his *Dreams With Silence* to a Brahms score, originally seen in Bournemouth in October. Although it inspired comparisons with his recent Scriabin ballet, critics noted that North's style was becoming increasingly classical in its use of a language to explore the emotions of a group.

The season had begun with a gala in aid of the scholarship fund and in a speech on this occasion Robert Cohan spoke of the need for funds to help support students otherwise denied the training they merited through the obduracy and meanness of education authorities, some of whom were unwilling even to fund one apprentice dancer.

Despite the range of the repertory and the number of creations in this season, the opinion was voiced that the company's technical skills were now outstripping the repertory. The standards of dancing were so high, the excellence of training so fruitful that no matter how numerous or varied the productions, they were not always stretching the dancers. As a tribute to Cohan's work, and evidence of the wide recognition he received, the Society of West End Theatre Managers annual award for 'outstanding achievement of the year in ballet' was given to him. Then known as the SWET Awards, the name has since been changed to the Olivier Awards.

1979

◆

January of 1979, the tenth anniversary year of the company, found LCDT in Rome. Two programmes, drawn from *Troy Game*, *Class*, *Sphinx*, *Scriabin Preludes*, *Stabat Mater* and *Forest*, were shown at the Teatro Olimpico, offering an attractive portrait of the company's achievement after a decade of endeavour. The physical power as well as the subtlety of the company's style could be seen in *Class*, *Troy Game* and *Forest*, as well as the evidence of choreography by two generations of creators already produced in the company's brief existence. There followed a flying visit to the *Journées Chorégraphiques de Toulouse* in mid-February, which was well received.

In March the Camden Festival again involved the company in a week of performances at the Collegiate Theatre which displayed works recently produced: Robert North's *Reflections*, originally made for Ballet Rambert in 1976; Anthony van Laast's evocation of Picasso acrobats, *Just Before*; Linda Gibbs dancing her own *Two Solos*; and Christopher Bannerman appearing with Sally Estep in his *Treading*. The company then mounted a four-week anniversary season at Sadler's Wells between 15 May and 9 June. The repertory offered nine works by Cohan, two by Micha Bergese, three by Siobhan Davies and four by Robert North, with, in the second week, a series of new creations from other members of the company. These continued to tell of LCDT's essential belief in creativity. Any retrospect of Contemporary Dance's activity over its decade of existence must acknowledge that it was the most productive ensemble in the history of British dance of any kind. Not even the extraordinary outpouring of work in the early days of Ballet Rambert can compare with this prodigality of new works. Whatever the standard of the pieces on show – and they were in the main very well crafted – the astonishing fact is that LCDT was prepared to give its dancers constant opportunities for making new work, and indeed expected them to create, even from their student days.

So it was that more new works were seen on 22 May: Tom Jobe's *Dance for Four* was a post-Cunningham exercise in which four girls were set moving to the sound of J. S. Bach's First Violin Sonata; Anthony van Laast's *Just Before* was repeated; Patrick Harding-Irmer's *Days Untold* was a solo in heroic style expressing spiritual aspiration and inquiry; Linda Gibbs' *Three Solos* used swirling piano music by Dudley James to send this fine dancer sweeping and flashing over the stage; Micha Bergese's *Scene Shift* was a work of dream-like illusion in which twelve white-clad dancers moved in illogical and quirky fashion that caught the imagination, as did the score by Carl Vine.

In the first two days of the next week yet more new works were on view. Christopher Bannerman's *Sand Steps* had initially appeared during the Collegiate Theatre season, and now its fluent dancing suggested different ways of moving on sand, responding to different textures. Cathy Lewis's *Kisses Remembered* was a duet for herself and Michael Small concerned with a tense and unhappy relationship; Anthony van Laast's *Through Blue* found three girls blithely dancing until a fourth joined them and disrupted the mood.

In his annual report at this time, summing up the past year, Robin Howard spoke with evident relief of the fact that 'The Trust has moved into most of its new buildings on the site adjoining The Place where we have been able to start some of the activities we have been planning for the last six years.' Audiences continued to rise despite the fact that the company had been able to relax its arduous touring schedule, and it was a matter for pride that during

Patrick Harding-Irmer with Christopher Bannerman, Michael Small and Robert North in Paul Taylor's Cloven Kingdom, *first staged by LCDT in 1979*

OVERPAGE: Songs, Lamentations and Praises *by Robert Cohan (1979)*

Christopher Bannerman and Cathy Lewis in Robert North's The Annunciation *(1979)*

the late autumn season at Sadler's Wells attendances topped 90% for half the programme.

Nevertheless, problems connected with such success remained. The work over-strained the dancers, 'particularly those who had had to tour for many years, who are also choreographers, or who have family responsibilities,' wrote Howard. He went on to identify a problem common to all British dance companies at this time: inflation had outstripped any rise in grant income, and there were depredations brought about by the Government's stringent wages policy. The cost of materials, of travel, of every aspect of the company's activities, had increased massively, but the dancers could not be recompensed in line with these increases.

The move into the new premises was also to facilitate community services, 'one of the Company's major activities', through the Education Extensions Department of the Contemporary Dance Trust. This programme, concerned with providing a good example of modern dance and good classes to achieve it, offered what the Trust called 'services' – teachers, speakers, films, walks round The Place, special demonstrations and the bringing of parties to compare performances. It was in effect seeking to stimulate and indoctrinate a young audience. Although the company was faced with financial cutbacks as part of an economic drive in the autumn of 1979, it yet contrived, as it had done throughout its history, to reach out for a new and youthful public and involve them, in as many ways as possible, with the life and identity of the company. The result has been that now, as then, a young and loyal audience has been fostered who see in London Contemporary Dance a company whom they love and trust. Anyone who has attended a performance of LCDT, in the regions as in London, will know that an essential and vociferous part of its public is made up of teenagers who respond with immediate delight to contemporary styles of movement.

At this time the company lost the services of Micha Bergese as dancer, though he was to continue to be associated with the Trust through his choreography.

The summer's travels took the company first, in mid-June, to the Holland Festival under the aegis of the British Council, performing to enthusiastic houses in Rotterdam, Scheveningen and Amsterdam. Then, between 2–8 August, they travelled to Israel for a first visit. LCDT had many links with this country: Robert Cohan had helped shape the first repertory of the Batsheva Company there in 1964, and had choreographed for that troupe and for the Bat-Dor ensemble; Moshe Romano, LCDT's associate director, had danced and worked with Batsheva for ten years before he joined LCDT in 1972. The occasion for this visit was an international seminar on The Bible in Dance. A large repertory was taken – *Khamsin*, *Diary 2*, *Class*, *Forest*, *Stabat Mater* – and on 7 August in the Jerusalem Theatre two brand new works were presented, Cohan's *Songs, Lamentations and Praises* and Robert North's *The Annunciation*, in a programme together with *Hunter of Angels* and *Stabat Mater*.

Songs, Lamentations and Praises, with a commissioned score from Geoffrey Burgon, explored the moods of Old Testament texts, taken from the Song of Songs and also the loss of Jerusalem, culminating in a final outburst of praise to God. *The Annunciation*, with a score by Howard Blake, told of the Annunciation and what Robert North identified as 'the sacrifices that will follow'. Additionally, on the final day of the visit, Robert Cohan showed a recording of his television production of *Job*.

The company returned to London to prepare for a new initiative – a season of dance 'in the round' at The Roundhouse in October. At the same time the enlarged premises at The Place were to become home to the Rambert School of Ballet, forced to move out of the Mercury Theatre which it had outgrown. Robin Howard, characteristically, came to the rescue at a time of crisis for this School. (Subsequently, in the early 1980s it merged with the Rambert Academy and moved into fine new studios at the West London College of Further Education at Twickenham.)

Also at this time LSCD gained a new principal in Dr Richard Ralph, who was to supervise a continued expansion of the School's academic activities, leading to the establishment of the degree course in dance in collaboration with the University of Kent.

The two weeks of dance at The Roundhouse from 2–13 October brought

the usual willingness to respond to fresh challenges. Three new works made up the programme, each seeking to overcome the directional diffuseness of dance in the round, and trying to reconcile an audience to the view of dancers from every angle rather than from the conventional and controlled 'straight-on' perspective. Siobhan Davies's *Ley Line* was a succession of dance incidents centred upon Philippe Giraudeau as a faun-like figure, but the choreography proved to be too self-centred to make much impact upon the public; Robert North's *Five Circular Studies* was a series of emotional duets from the choreographer and Sally Estep which spread over the dance area without self-consciousness; Robert Cohan's *Rondo* was a set of six variations to a strong score by John Herbert McDowell in which the dancers marked out the limits of the arena before more intense activities occupied the central area. The feeling was of ritual, of generous movement filling the space with no sense of blind spots and it brought an outstanding performance by Patrick Harding-Irmer in a leaping solo that gripped the audience. This experiment was repeated between 17–20 October in performances at the Hexagon Theatre, Reading, well suited to presentations in the round.

After a short regional tour the Company returned to Sadler's Wells for its autumn season between 27 November and 8 December. The Biblical works already seen in Israel were to be the novelties of the repertory together with one important acquisition, Paul Taylor's *Cloven Kingdom*. This sardonic study of the beast under the skin was done with a notable sense of its style, and it brought exceptionally rewarding performances from Anca Frankenhaeuser and Siobhan Davies, and from a male quartet of Patrick Harding-Irmer, Michael Small, Robert North and Christopher Bannerman, who rejoiced in the grotesque capers and brutalisms of the male writing.

Kate Harrison in Christopher Bannerman's Sand Steps *(1979)*

1980

◆

'1979/80 was dominated by problems arising from the expansion of The Place.' Thus noted Robin Howard in his annual report, continuing with the news that unexpected delays and expenses had caused a dangerous financial situation. Yet, even given these delays, The Place as headquarters of Dance School, Trust and Company was, in Howard's view 'the envy of much of the dance world'. The financial problems related to escalating costs and unforeseen increases in labour and materials. 'The building work eventually cost £554,974, an increase of more than two-thirds of the contract figure of £332,000 agreed only 14 months earlier. At the same time, there was a loss in school numbers, which cost us £56,000 over the full year. The resulting position, in layman's terms, was that on March 31, 1980 the Trust owed £667,706 or in round pounds a quarter of a million more than we anticipated.' As a result there was a reduction in many ancillary activities, including educational work, and 'during 1980–81 our cash flow problem was made worse by the fact that on November 30, 1980 local education authorities owed us £71,600 which should have been paid before the new term started in September.'

In November two properties belonging to Robin Howard and the Trust were auctioned and produced £70,000. Expenditure on building work was halted. Nevertheless, the activities of the company and school were to proceed as normal – and even adventurously – as the year progressed.

In May, dancers in the company made a report to the executive committee of the Trust suggesting a division of activities which, in addition to full scale seasons by the whole company, would allow the dancers 'to work in a new way, with a more flexible yet structured situation with workshops presented at The Place. One or two experienced choreographers could work with a group of dancers and perform their work at The Place and in different venues throughout Britain. Other dancers may want to take off or want to perform or teach elsewhere.' These and other ideas were intended to take the company into new areas while still capitalising on the strengths built up over the previous decade. Robin Howard was in sympathy with the idea, and it is the financial problems which could be seen as a reason for inhibiting realisation of the proposed strategy.

Certainly the early months of the year brought enterprising work. In a project scheduled for five weeks during January and February, the residencies scheme operated at Wakeford School, Havant, Hampshire with dancers from the com-

Linda Gibbs and Robert North in North's Death and the Maiden *(1980)*

pany sharing duties in class and sessions of apprentice choreography with the school's pupils. Meanwhile LCDT again split into two groups for three weeks to cover a spring tour of southern England with Micha Bergese directing one section of the company, Robert North the other. New creations were produced: Tom Jobe's *One*, Robert North's *Death and the Maiden*, Micha Bergese's *Some Dance and Some Duet*, and Robert Cohan's *Field*. Janet Smith joined the company for this tour and Darshan Singh Bhuller, still a student, also appeared. At The Place a group of students from the School took part in an evening of choreography by Richard Alston which showed these fresh, youthful dancers in fresh, youthful dances set to Dvorak's Dumky Trio.

But in this year of crises, a crisis loomed for the School. By May, it was clear that discretionary grants would not be forthcoming for several aspirant students at The Place, and a press conference was called on 27 May to alert the public to the problems. These related both to the delay in local education authorities announcing the grants that would be available and also to the cutting down of discretionary funding and the impossibility of the School obtaining mandatory grants. As the press hand-out from Jack Norton, for many years the financial director of the Trust and an architect of its success, stated about the School: 'it would have few financial problems if it shared the benefits of capital support and mandatory granting . . . Its continuing progress and the promising careers of the many brilliant young dancers are threatened by a phase of unprecedented financial restraint.'

An appeal fund was launched to raise £50,000 in an attempt to stave off possible closure. As Richard Ralph, Director of the School, told the *Daily Telegraph*: 'The bleak prospect is that England may lose not only its foremost contemporary dance school but its finest contemporary dance company.' Thus it was that private sponsorship was sought to guarantee some security for prospective students and for the School itself. It was ironic that at a time when the annual report could note that 'The faculty estimates that the School lost 17 applicants of more than usual promise, many of whom have now decided to abandon dance altogether', a report commissioned by the Gulbenkian Foundation could give nothing but the highest praise for the work of the School: 'one of the most important developments in British dance education since the war'.

Despite these many problems LCDT embarked upon its longest tour of Europe in June, under the auspices of the British Council, with scheduled visits to eight countries. The tour began in splendid style with two sold-out weeks at the Théâtre de la Ville in Paris. Thence the company visited Lausanne, the Maggio Musicale in Florence, Cyprus, Athens, the Istanbul Festival, the Carinthian Summer Festival at Villach, Dubrovnik and Ljubljana.

Impressive as the tour was, it was not without incident. Janet Eager recollects that the company was scheduled to travel from Cyprus to Turkey, but political tensions made a direct flight impossible. Hence the journey was to be from Limassol to Athens, with a change for the onward journey to Istanbul which would take them to Alexandropolis in Northern Greece and thence by special coach into Turkey. The company left Limassol early on Sunday morning and as Janet Eager climbed up the stairs on to the plane she was given a message to say that Olympic Airlines was on strike and that by the time they reached Athens further travel would be impossible. Athens airport was chaotic. Janet Eager had to go from one airline desk to the next in vain search for a flight. Eventually, Bulgarian Airlines was able to offer the use of a bus which would take the company to Alexandropolis. It would not leave until late in the afternoon and, while she arranged for the dancers to spend a day on the beach, Janet Eager herself had hurriedly to rustle up £600 in cash in order to pay for the coach – no easy task on a Sunday. Eventually she succeeded, organised transport to and from the beach for the dancers and booked an hotel for them in Salonika where they would spend the night. Telephone communication with the authorities in Istanbul was impossible on a Sunday but fortunately she was able to contact the British Council's representative, Val West, in London who, in turn, could arrange for the coach to meet the company on the Greek/Turkish border to take them on to Istanbul.

The Bulgarian coach, promised as air-conditioned, proved to be cramped and to possess only two small electric fans by the driver. Nevertheless, through the heat of a late summer day, they travelled to Salonika, arriving there at 3.30 in the morning. Five hours later, they set off again for Alexandropolis – where the driver stopped. He refused to go any further and it was only after anguished telephone calls that he was allowed to drive them to the border, at which prospect he disappeared totally for an hour. He returned looking very sleek in appearance, because he had decided to have a shave and a haircut – so as not to disgrace LCDT. Eventually the border was reached and there were further complications. The driver was without a visa and could not cross. But there, in the distance, was the anticipated Turkish coach. Janet Eager had to run the gauntlet of some menacing guards to arrange for the new coach to back right up to the border and then bring the dancers across this no-man's land burdened with their luggage, and with Namron further laden with part of the touring set which they had been obliged to bring with them.

While the company was on this tour, their work was being seen by a large British audience thanks to BBC Television. June was 'Dance Month' on BBC TV, with a wide and excellent variety of dance programmes. With justifiable pride, the Trust declared that the most popular master class had been that given by Robert Cohan and the most popular of the ballet recordings – which had included the Kirov Ballet, the Martha Graham Company and the Royal Ballet – was a double bill of Cohan's *Forest* and *Waterless Method of Swimming Instruction.*

Regional touring began after the summer break and it is curious to record that at this time LCDT could play to a dispiriting 32% capacity in Leeds but drew a near-full 94% in Exeter. At the Theatre Clwyd in Mold, the company gave the first performances of Christopher Bannerman's *The Singing*, inspired by the poetry of Walt Whitman, and Siobhan Davies's exercise in dance conversation, *Something to Tell*.

The financial crisis was in no way abated, and a fund raising letter was sent out signed by the grandest names of the balletic establishment: Sir Frederick Ashton, Anton Dolin, Dame Margot Fonteyn, Dame Alicia Markova, Rudolf Nureyev, Dame Marie Rambert, and Dame Ninette de Valois. They rallied to the support of the School: 'There is no comparable contemporary dance organisation in the world; its twin enterprises, London Contemporary Dance Theatre and London School of Contemporary Dance, have a unique international reputation. The work of the Trust is vital to the artistic life of Britain and brings immense credit to us abroad. It needs and deserves your support.'

The letter also identified the commendation given to the Trust by the recently-published report of the Gulbenkian Foundation which had taken four years to compile from information provided by the leading authorities in dance and education. All stressed the need for financial assistance. Perhaps the most telling comment came in the closing phrase of the appeals letter itself: 'Young dancers can not wait for training; once they miss the chance it is gone for ever.' Alas, despite its prestigious signatories, the letter brought in virtually no money.

As the autumn season got under way the Trust announced significant changes in the administration and running of the company. Janet Eager, the administrator of the company and Robert North, associate choreographer, were named as associate directors and Robert North was announced as taking charge of the company during the early months of 1981 when Robert Cohan was to take extended sabbatical leave. The forthcoming year was to be important in any case as it would bring the company to the Edinburgh Festival for the first time. The recently inaugurated Tennant Caledonian Award for the creation of a new work at the Festival had been given to LCDT for 1981 to enable the company to create a dance work and to continue its policy of residencies there. Although the sum of £20,000 was not a fortune, it did provide working capital for a major work for the following year.

The autumn tour culminated in the regular season at the Wells, which opened with a benefit performance for the scholarship fund on 18 November. The programme included the first showing of Robert Cohan's *Field*, and *If My Complaints Should Passion Move* (a suitable title for a gala appealing for funds) made by Siobhan Davies to be performed by the students of the School.

Field was a nature study ballet, something after the fashion of *Forest* if less convincing in delineating people moving across a space, the choreography catching them on and off balance. Another London premiere was Siobhan Davies's *Something to Tell*, which proved less than engrossing in its quest to present 'several conversations as in a play, which follow the musical structure'. The score was by Benjamin Britten, his Third Cello Suite and his Variations on Russian Folk Songs, and a principal couple, Siobhan Davies and Robert North, were shown as hosts to a group of friends. There were hints of passions about to let fly, but nothing in the work suggested what they were: at curtain fall the audience was left still anticipating that tensions would explode. Of the other pieces new to London Christopher Bannerman's *The Singing* showed four duets emerging from the relationships between three couples, with the most stimulating writing given to the choreographer himself and Patrick Harding-Irmer. The dance developed from simple pushing gestures into leaps which found the two men dashing past each other and then bringing the duet to a resolution with a simple embrace.

Robert North's *Death and the Maiden* awoke memories for the older members of the audience of Andrée Howard's setting of part of the same Schubert music more than forty years before for Ballet Rambert. North took the first two movements of the quartet, concentrating the emotion in the second movement – the variations on the song – in which Linda Gibbs as the Maiden danced with radiant simplicity and grace while Death (Robert North) marked her out with grotesque, expressionistic movement. Anca Frankenhaeuser was the other principal, as a consoling mother figure of touching compassion.

1981

◆

At the beginning of 1981 Robin Howard produced a review of the Trust's policies and a forecast which touched on many aspects of its work. He observed that the Trust was now organised into six operational units – the School, the Dance Company, the Evening School, the Children's and Teenage Dances, the Educational Extension and Community Work, and The Place itself. He noted: 'That we have been successful in our original intentions is now a matter of record.' As some comment upon the School there was the fact that a degree course in dance, bruited for some time, now seemed likely to be realised within a year; speaking of the Company, he made reference to the privately commissioned report made six years before by Gail Law. Law, a greatly admired dance administrator, had produced a preliminary report about the Dance Theatre in October 1974 and following it two years later with a 'final report'. In Robin Howard's words, 'The main conclusion of Mr Law's most recent document was that LCDT was a new kind of dance company, the "creative company" which is a permanent dance company engaged in a continual state of creativity and exploratory activity, the product of which is made available to the public in performance.'

The proposed developments and the re-organisation were not to interfere with the round of touring which found LCDT in Exeter at the beginning of February. Here the first performance was given of Robert North's *Songs and Dances*, to Schubert music. The choreography was divided between 'out of doors', which was pastoral to a quartet movement, and 'indoors', in which a group of songs – including the famous 'Serenade' and 'The Earl King' – were interpreted in dramatic terms. This was to be Robert North's last creation as a member of the company for, at the end of March, after fourteen years' service as dancer and choreographer, he was appointed Director of Ballet Rambert. The company suffered further loss also at this time – though it was envisaged by company policy – when Siobhan Davies took sabbatical leave in order to work with a small group of her own dancers.

The tour brought a gratifying visit to Liverpool, as the annual report indicated. 'For the first time in five years it was decided to re-visit Liverpool, the large Empire Theatre with 2,000 seats but using the stalls only (1,100 seats). In the event, the performances were so popular that the Dress Circle had to be opened on two evenings. After such a long period away from this centre, we were most heartened by this result.'

The return to London in April and May was to The Place for a series of work-

Philip Taylor in his own solo
The Home Run *(1981)*

142

*Philip Taylor and Charlotte
Kirkpatrick in Robert North's*
Songs and Dances *(1981)*

Lizie Saunderson and Michael Small in Darshan Singh Bhuller's Beyond the Law *(1981)*

shop performances. The departure of Robert North and the absence on leave of Robert Cohan and Siobhan Davies did not reduce the company's creativity during this period of three weeks when four new works were shown. Christopher Bannerman's *Danger, Work in Progress* was a collaborative work produced by Bannerman and members of the company in which the disruptive dance action sought to mirror the problems of creativity. Darshan Singh Bhuller's *Beyond the Law* was an angry comment upon the race legislation in South Africa. Jayne Lee's *Recall* was a study in unhappy memories, and Philip Taylor's *Home Run* was a joke about a baseball player.

With this season over, the company returned to touring and to working with Robert Cohan on his new, large piece which would mark the company's appearance at the Edinburgh Festival. *Dances of Love and Death* was due to be staged in the Moray House Gymnasium on 31 August. The Tennant Caledonian Award allowed Cohan to create on the same scale as he had done a decade earlier with *Stages*. The new piece was concerned with narrative itself and the way in which stories are told and remembered. Since historical modern dance had usually been concerned with the inner world of its characters, it was a radical undertaking to devote an evening to the idea of concise narration. Cohan made his point by choosing five celebrated love stories whose unifying theme is the conflict between love and death. He showed Love (a role created by Celia Hulton) and Death (Tom Jobe) as manipulators of the action, while an additional theme

was the irreducible minimum of a story which remains in the public memory. Hence each of the work's five scenes was brief and separated from the others by unrelated interludes of what might be thought of as party chatter – performed to the piano-roll studies of Conlon Nancarrow while the score for the main episodes was provided by Carl Davis. The narratives were those of the Rape of Persephone, Tristan and Iseult, the Sleeping Beauty, Cathy and Heathcliffe, and Marilyn Monroe. Performances were very strong from the entire company and the piece was markedly successful with the Edinburgh audience.

From the Festival, the company travelled to the Eastern bloc under the sponsorship of the British Council, appearing in Poland at Lodz and Warsaw to great acclaim. The return to Britain and to touring brought the first performance of Siobhan Davies's *Free Setting* at Warwick University on 15 October. In a programme note the choreographer told how the composer (Michael Finnissy) and the designer (David Buckland) 'gave me their plans three months before I began the work and these thoughts helped discipline my own ideas. In order to find the movement, I used word associations which refer to the title *Free Setting*.' The result was a dance work clear-textured and elegantly lucid: the score by Michael Finnissy, with its alternating cascades of notes and sections of stillness, was admirably performed by Eleanor Alberga, who had joined the company the year before and was to become invaluable both as pianist and composer.

The autumn brought nearer the possibility of the re-opening of The Place

Celia Hulton in Robert Cohan's Dances of Love and Death *(1981)*

Celia Hulton as Marilyn Monroe in Dances of Love and Death

Theatre as a public theatre after a lengthy closure (except for LCDT purposes). A grant under the Urban Aid Scheme meant that much-needed refurbishment could be undertaken to meet the standard prescribed by a Public Entertainments Licence. Further work remained to be done though, and the theatre was not to re-open for performances for another year. Sadler's Wells remained, of course, the company's London showcase and it was here that LCDT's winter season began on 17 November, continuing for four weeks.

The year's creations by Cohan, Davies and the young talents of the May workshops were on view as was a programme of Robert North choreographies in a gesture of recognition of his work for the company: *Troy Game, Death and the Maiden*, and *Songs and Dances*.

1982

◆

The continuing importance of residencies was clearly identified in the annual report:

> Our Rhonda Valley project, which offered lecture demonstration performances to more than 600 fifth and sixth formers, most of whom had seen little or no live theatre dance before, proved extremely successful. In January and February this year the company provided a four week residency in four secondary schools in Hampshire, with one week of performances, teaching and open sessions in each school. Teachers and musicians remained to give continuity. At the end of the period, the schools presented to each other and to their parents something of the work that had been achieved, which was received with extraordinary enthusiasm by teachers, advisers, dancers, musicians and by the children themselves. We have received sponsorship from the National Westminster Bank, which will allow us to run a small group of about six dancers for three months to offer lecture demonstrations in schools and community centres. Granted more assistance, we would hope to continue this activity.

In a report covering the year 1982–3, Richard Mansfield, the Trust's officer for education and community services, could cite more than 120 classes and workshops taught by members of the company to an estimated 3,600 schoolchildren and teenagers, centred mainly round the inner city areas of Liverpool, Leeds, Newcastle upon Tyne, Glasgow, Birmingham, Oxford, Leicester, Southampton, Cardiff, Bristol, Edinburgh and London. Special matinees introduced LCDT and its work to 15,000 young people (three matinees at Sadler's Wells 'were crammed full') and no fewer than 18,000 copies of a booklet sponsored by BP, *Introduction to LCDT*, were given away to the young. Further, a series of days with LCDT around the country brought up to forty young people a day to visit the theatre where the company was working, to join in classes and workshops based on LCDT's repertory, watch rehearsals and class, visit backstage and see the performance.

This characteristically broad policy of encouraging a new audience by direct and wholehearted involvement with the work and the identity of the company was further developed in succeeding years. It was, and remains at the time of writing, a central fact of the company's beliefs and like every other aspect of the Trust's work it would suffer from financial constraints. The 1981/82 annual report from Robin Howard to the Board declared 'In terms of income we find ourselves in a Red Queen situation. The company's takings have increased considerably, but not in the profitability of touring, where theatres have had to put up their charges even more than anticipated in their own fight for survival. Next year, however hard we run it will be difficult to stand still economically.'

Company life nevertheless continued with the spring taken up by regional touring, and in Exeter in February a work by the American dancer Richard Kuch was mounted. *The Brood* was based on Brecht's *Mother Courage*. It had earlier been seen in Britain in performance with Les Grands Ballets Canadiens, and now it was mounted for the younger members of LCDT who performed it with a dedication which was not sufficient, however, to make it seem a notable acquisition. The spring tour by a medium-sized company (certain senior LCDT members were on sabbatical leave) allowed Patrick Harding-Irmer to serve as acting artistic director, and it was followed by six weeks of performances which brought *Dances of Love and Death* to major cities in the regions with a total audience of nearly 29,000 people and a 60% average capacity, a fine record at a time of financial problems for theatres and public alike. During the early summer Siobhan Davies took further leave of absence in order to work with Second Stride, a new experimental company which planned to visit America and the Edinburgh Festival, and she was joined in this sabbatical by Philippe Giraudeau who had emerged as a very valuable and elegant member of the company. One other dancer left the troupe at this time. After seventeen years yeoman service Namron, who had been one of the early students in the 1960s, retired from the stage though he would continue to be associated with the Trust.

By August the company was at The Place preparing two weeks of company workshops, in which eleven dancers produced new pieces of choreography. One of these, Tom Jobe's *Liquid Assets*, entered the company repertory for the major adventure of the autumn, the troupe's first visit to Canada. But before this there came another 'first' for the Trust: the establishment of a BA honours degree in contemporary dance, validated by the University of Kent at Canterbury. It made concrete the aspirations of the Trust and of the School under its principal Richard Ralph, who had been instrumental in fulfilling this remarkable academic achievement. This was, he wrote:

the first university honours degree for professional dancers in Europe . . . like the degrees which can be gained in Art Schools, whereby the degree-worthy element is predominantly practical. In this case it breaks down to 72% practical work, 14% contexts of dance (music, stagecraft, anatomy), and 14% more academic study in Theatre History, Human Biology, etc. The degree is entirely taught in house, with visiting tutors for the theoretical work. There has been a teaching arrangement with the Royal College of Art to cover some of the first year work as well. The first year graduating class (graduating in 1985) included three part-time degree students from LCDT who had taken a two

Patrick Harding-Irmer and Darshan Singh Bhuller in Richard Kuch's The Brood, *as staged for London Contemporary Dance Theatre in 1982*

Michael Small and Sally Estep in Robert Cohan's Chamber Dances *(1982)*

year variant of the course. They have exactly the same examination in all subjects, but take only the theoretical class work. These three students all gained first class honours degrees: Patrick Harding-Irmer, Anca Frankenhaeuser, and Charlotte Kirkpatrick.

Six other full-time students also took the first course.

Robert Cohan believes that this BA honours degree is enormously significant for school and company since the students must have sufficient artistic and technical status as well as academic ability to work in the public sector. In the United States many contemporary dancers have been to college and obtained a first degree. It is entirely unfair that in Britain, heretofore, a talent to dance has meant a choice between a dance career and a degree. It is a praiseworthy achievement that, thanks to LCDT, these two halves of a personality have been reconciled.

While this academic year got under way, and the Trust relaunched a scheme of children's and teenagers' classes at The Place under the new title of The Young Place, LCDT went out on a regional tour which saw the first performance of Cohan's *Chamber Dances* in Southampton on 16 September. With an attractive score by Geoffrey Burgon, six couples were seen in relationships that suggested lovers' meetings, with a gradual darkening of the mood initiated by an incantatory solo for Patrick Harding-Irmer, its curious steppings and turns having an almost ritualistic air. The nearest the dance came to any overt statement of feeling was in the arrival of Charlotte Kirkpatrick, swathed in a vast blue cloak which became a habitation for the men of the ensemble who were caught in its folds. The work's resolution found its couples restored to a freer and happier mode of dancing and the piece drew excellently strong performances from its ensemble.

Two days before the company had also given its first performance, in Southampton, of Paul Taylor's *Esplanade*. Mounted for the company by Eileen Cropley, *Esplanade* suited the power and athleticism of LCDT's cast very well: they rejoiced in this dazzling Taylorian conceit which shows non-dance – running, falling, walking, every mode of movement except dancing – as dancing.

Then from 10 October to 8 November the company set out on the conquest of Canada; a four-week visit to Toronto, Ottawa, Montreal, Trois Rivières, Quebec, Sherbrooke, Banff, Edmonton and Vancouver, under the auspices of the Canada Council and the British Council, which was by way of being a triumphal progress across the country. Notices were uniformly ecstatic. The repertory included *Class*, *Stabat Mater*, *Forest*, *Rainbow Bandit*, *Death and the Maiden*, *Free Setting*, a duet from *Nymphéas*, and a creation for the tour from the Canadian-born Christopher Bannerman. His *Second Turning* was inspired, as its programme note declared, by the choreographer's feelings on returning to dance in Canada after ten years: 'My thoughts naturally turned to the events of the intervening years, as well as the relentless movement of time.'

The company's reception was everywhere of the happiest, Canadian critics vying with each other in heaping praise on the ensemble. 'London dancers hold audience in rapture,' wrote Max Wyman in Vancouver. 'I've rarely seen Vancouver audiences so rapt.' William Littler in the *Toronto Star* recorded that 'a collective whoop' went up from the audience at the end of the Canadian debut performance by LCDT, while another critic simply declared the troupe to be 'overwhelming'.

The company's return to Britain took them to London for their Sadler's Wells season. The repertory surveyed the year's creations by Cohan and Christopher Bannerman, and Tom Jobe's joking *Liquid Assets* (which had been seen in the May workshops). Revivals included *Rainbow Bandit*, with Linda Gibbs beautifully back in its cast, after a season dancing in the musical *Song and Dance*, and works by Siobhan Davies and Robert North, with Paul Taylor's *Esplanade* performed with a fine comprehension of its style. The company was dancing superbly well, buoyed up by the triumphs of Canada and seemingly untried by the demands of the tour. As Alastair Macaulay wrote in the *Dancing Times* about this season: 'If you want to see immaculate execution of dance technique, LCDT is the shop for it. As a dance machine it can't be topped in Britain today.'

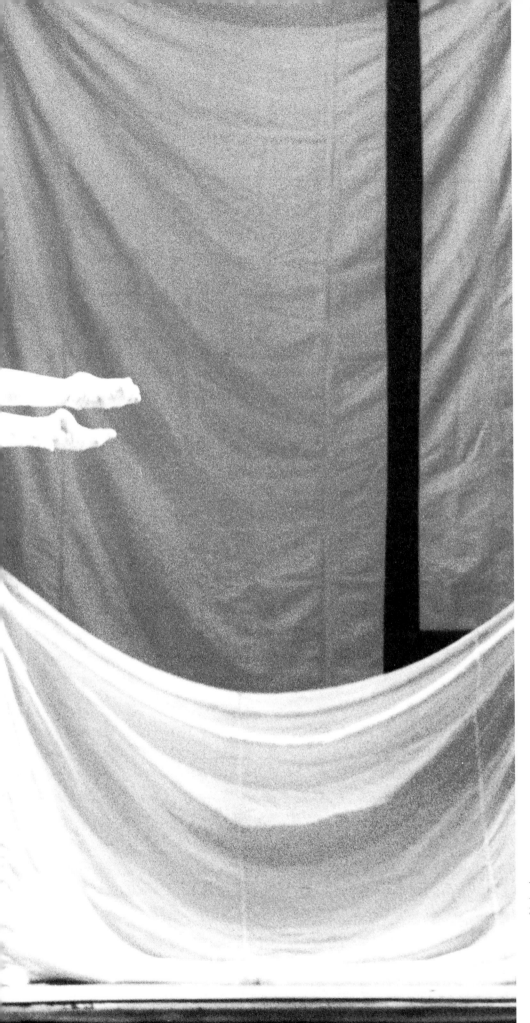

Lauren Potter and Christopher Bannerman in the latter's Second Turning *(1982)*

1983

◆

At the beginning of 1983 LCDT was again able to reach out to a national audience through the medium of television when, on 29 January, BBC TV transmitted Robert Cohan's *Cell*, with the additional benefit of an introduction by the choreographer. At this time the company was on a major regional tour visiting Oxford (where Siobhan Davies's new *The Dancing Department* was given its first performance on 8 February), Leeds, Birmingham, Liverpool, Glasgow and Edinburgh. *The Dancing Department* was set to Bach's 'Musical Offering' and it borrowed certain formal attitudes from the music's devices.

Meanwhile the Education and Community Department of the Trust began two important educational innovations, the 'Days with LCDT' and 'The Touring Workshop Unit' which were sponsored by National Westminster Bank. Both these projects enabled young people to come into much closer contact with the company and its ideals. In the Days with LCDT as many as thirty-five young people, together with their teachers or youth leaders, were brought together with the company throughout a whole day, watching class and rehearsals, joining in practical sessions with dancers and staff and finally seeing an evening performance. The building of an audience in this fashion was indicative both of the imaginative approach of the Trust and also of the fundamental idealism which guided all its activities. The Touring Workshop was able to visit schools, colleges and youth clubs, taking practical classes and the residency ideal directly to the prospective audience who were also able to experience the company in performance.

May brought what must seem the final accolade on the Howard/Cohan enterprise when, as part of the 'Britain Salutes New York' Festival, LCDT was invited to appear at the Brooklyn Academy of Music between 3 and 8 May. The visit was presaged by financial difficulties. As Robin Howard stated in the annual report 'we nearly had to refuse the invitation to perform in New York. It was only thanks to sponsorship from the British Council, British Airways, Morgan Guaranty Trust Company and, especially, Wedgwood Inc., and an extra grant from the Britain Salutes New York Committee itself, that the visit was able to take place.' But the visit did take place and the success was overwhelming. It was heartening to read the review by Clive Barnes in the *New York Post*, especially since Barnes had been of exceptional help in fostering the company in its earliest days. Now as a critic in New York, he could write: 'As I left the theatre, it seemed as though the whole house was cheering. It is the kind of

Patrick Harding-Irmer with Charlotte Kirkpatrick and Anca Frankenhaeuser in Siobhan Davies's The Dancing Department *(1983). Photograph by David Buckland*

159

Celia Hulton in Jayne Lee's
Spinnaker *(1983)*

Members of the company in The Dancing Department. *Photograph by David Buckland*

success that can be compared with the initial impact of the Royal Ballet in New York in 1949. In those days New York hardly suspected that Britain had any classic dancers and was mightily surprised. Last night, we found Britain now also has superb modern-dancers . . . They are just terrific dancers.'

The other New York critics seemed no less appreciative of the dancing and the repertory was respected for its variety: the company took as a first programme *Nymphéas*, *The Dancing Department* and *Class* and, for its second programme, *Death and the Maiden* (Robert North rejoining the company to appear in his own work), *Liquid Assets*, *Forest* and *Cell*.

The company returned from New York to prepare itself for a very significant London season at Sadler's Wells later in May. This was to mark the retirement from the sole leadership of the company of Robert Cohan. The season began on 23 May with a repertory bill: then came a royal gala in the presence of Princess Alexandra on 26 May which had, as the programme noted, two purposes: 'to pay tribute to Robert Cohan, who later this year will relinquish his post as full-time artistic director of London Contemporary Dance Theatre, which he has held for 17 years; to launch the Trust's major Fund Raising Campaign.' In a tribute to Cohan, Peter Williams, whose support for the Trust had itself been of inestimable value through his work with the Arts Council and as editor of *Dance* and *Dancers*, wrote 'It is one thing to introduce new and developing art forms, especially in a country so classical-ballet orientated as was Britain up

Anita Griffin and Michael Small in Tom Jobe's Run Like Thunder *(1983). Photograph by David Buckland*

until the early 1950s, but it takes someone with a unique personality to make it all work in a way that can eventually change a whole nation's attitude towards dance . . . In its way, his contribution to the whole dance scene in Britain parallels that of those two other legendary pioneers – Dames Ninette de Valois and Marie Rambert.' The gala programme contained three of Cohan's major works, *Stabat Mater*, *Class* and *Forest*, and the season ended with a revival of his *Dances of Love and Death*.

In the belief that Heaven and sponsors (and Esso had sponsored the gala) help those who help themselves, Robin Howard also decided to sell at auction costumes from the Diaghilev Ballet that he had bought at sales a decade before – the proceeds of this sale to go to the Contemporary Dance Trust.

Robert Cohan's decision to cut down on his work with the company inevitably seemed traumatic, but in the event the separation was less severe than this. The company having searched widely but in vain for a successor, he agreed to serve for seven months of the year as an artistic adviser and in August 1983 a triumvirate of directors was established, with Robert Cohan being responsible for artistic policy, Siobhan Davies becoming resident choreographer, and Janet Eager continuing as adminstrator.

On their return from their summer holidays the company paid a brief visit to the Helsinki Festival, dancing at the Finlandia Hall on 10 and 11 September. Thereafter the company set out on a regional tour which brought the creation of three new works during the season in Leicester: Jayne Lee's *Spinnaker* and Darshan Singh Bhuller's *Under the Same Sun* were shown on 20 September, while Tom Jobe's *Run Like Thunder* was first seen two days later.

Spinnaker was inspired by movements taken from sailing; *Under the Same Sun* was concerned with Indian religious experience and offered some ebullient dances for three men and two women. *Run Like Thunder* was an obvious crowd pleaser with its bright disco-frantic dances matching the energies of the score by Barrington Pheloung, LCDT's musical director.

In October the company also went to participate in the Dublin Theatre Festival, appearing at the Gaiety Theatre between 4 and 8 October – their first visit to Eire. The repertory of *Run Like Thunder*, *Stabat Mater* and *Class* was immediately attractive and understandably excited the Irish audience.

A new work entered the repertory on the company's return to a regional tour when Christopher Bannerman's *Canso Trobar* was seen at the Warwick University Arts Centre on 20 October. Its text used Provençal songs, and the dance responded both to the jovial pipings and drumming played on instruments of the medieval period, and to the more serious and sensual attitudes of courtly love.

These four new pieces all featured in the Sadler's Wells season, which ran from 22 November until 10 December. One further novelty was the first performance, on 6 December, of Siobhan Davies's *Carnival of the Animals* which had been created the year before for Second Stride. Designed by David Buckland

and Antony McDonald, *Carnival* had a pretty backdrop, which showed Saint Saëns gazing at the audience from a Douanier Rousseau jungle, and ingenious choreography which explored the characteristics of the music. It was a work memorable especially for two roles taken by Philippe Giraudeau, who had returned to the company from appearances with Second Stride for this season. As a timid lover whose automatic and unavailing gesture, hand to heart, matched the Cuckoo's call, he was all pathos, a tragic Stan Laurel. As the Swan, he was the incarnation both of the bird and the cello soloist, and his performance seemed to many observers, not least the present writers, to be touched with greatness.

As a final contact with a huge audience that year, the BBC transmitted a recording of *Nymphéas* (excellently directed, as had been *Cell*, by Bob Lockyer) on 9 December and the programme was seen by an audience estimated at 900,000 viewers.

Sally Estep and Darshan Singh Bhuller in Christopher Bannerman's Canso Trobar *(1984)*

1984

◆

The performing year of 1984 began in February with a visit to Leeds. After a period of rehearsals, two new works were ready for presentation at the Grand Theatre: Siobhan Davies's *New Galileo* and Robert Cohan's *Agora*. *New Galileo*, first given on 14 February, was a plotless work set to a minimalist piano score by John Adams, superbly played by Eleanor Alberga. The stage was divided into three lateral sections by means of spidery gantries carrying light battens. Behind them were skewed panels showing a dancer in a studio, birds, and a disc, which gradually came into focus as the action progressed. The work was very cerebral and the gradual spreading of the gantries across the stage marked an increase in the energy of the dance. Despite its intellectual air, the work was impressively performed especially by its male contingent of Patrick Harding-Irmer, Jonathan Lunn, Darshan Singh Bhuller and Michael Small.

Two days later Cohan's response to a Bach score and a sound collage by Barrington Pheloung was *Agora*, whose final section, to the sixth Brandenburg Concerto, inspired a grand and energetic response from its cast.

After visits to Liverpool and Oxford and some workshops in London directed by Siobhan Davies, the company paid a brief visit to Barcelona between 29 April and 5 May as part of a spring dance festival at the Liceo Theatre, a visit which, as Robin Howard wrote in his annual report, gave the company 'the satisfaction of enthusiastic audience response, excellent reviews, and takings which paid for our expenses.'

One slight incident threatened the season, however. Janet Eager received a telegram just before the company was due to set out announcing that Monserrat Caballe wished to sing there on her birthday. Janet Eager flew to Barcelona and agreed that LCDT would build their season around Madame Caballe's birthday recital and she further ensured that the company would be able to attend the concert to hear the diva. The return to London was for a short season at Sadler's Wells from 15 May to 26 May when the repertory included *Canso Trobar*, *New Galileo*, *Songs*, *Lamentations and Praises*, *Agora*, *Carnival* and *Run Like Thunder*. The season was well received but proved a box office disappointment, not least because both the Royal Ballet and the Moscow Classical Ballet had concurrent seasons and the National Ballet of Cuba had lately finished a London visit.

From the Wells, the company went to Norway where it gave two performances at the Bergen Festival, then to Gothenburg in Sweden for three performances,

Jonathan Lunn in Siobhan Davies's New Galileo *(1984). Photograph by David Buckland*

and then back to America for two prestigious engagements – at the American Dance Festival, which was celebrating its 50th anniversary in Durham, North Carolina, and at Los Angeles where the Olympic Games were being marked by associated artistic performances.

It was a tribute to the international reputation of LCDT that it should fly the banner of British dance at the unique celebrations marking the Los Angeles Olympics. The company was seen at the Pasadena Civic Auditorium on 26 and 27 June with two programmes. Earlier it had been honoured in no less signal fashion by the invitation to join the 50th anniversary celebrations of the American Dance Festival – which could trace an extraordinary history of innovative contemporary dance from its earliest days in Bennington, Vermont, through later manifestations at New London, Connecticut, to its present home at Durham University.

Robin Howard described these visits as 'artistic landmarks' in the company's history.

After the summer holidays the company returned to regional touring in Britain and at the Derngate Theatre in Northampton, at the start of its autumn journeys, it produced two new works – Robert Cohan's *Skyward* and Tom Jobe's *Rite Electrik*. *Skyward* was danced to Eleanor Alberga's piano work *Clouds* and found its theme in the activities of the common European lark which when in danger 'soars towards the sky in a vertical flight path'. The choreography showed the cast at first nestling in the ground and then gradually becoming more active and airborne. A set of tubular metal which gradually rose obliquely above the stage in Norberto Chiesa's design helped give the illusion of flight.

There could be no greater contrast than Tom Jobe's *Rite Electrik* which was as abrasively up to date as the disco life it portrayed. The cast of six girls and four boys were dressed in studded, leather-look bondage gear, the score by Barrington Pheloung was a Concerto for Saxophone with whiplash percussion accompaniment played live on stage by Dale Barlow. The action was more than ambivalent, with the characters strutting and parading in a courtship ritual that was a telling portrait of contemporary morals in a certain section of society. The piece had a hectic energy and was immensely popular with young audiences.

As was by now customary, the autumn season at Sadler's Wells between 20 November and 8 December brought all the new repertory to the London audience, together with a notable acquisition of Richard Alston's *Doublework*. Originally created for Alston's own group at Riverside Studios in 1978, when it was performed in silence, it was a sequence of cool and carefully wrought duets whose effects were not here enhanced by the acquisition of a score by James Fulkerson. The season was a continuing exploration of the company's dance abilities and the *Dancing Times* found the troupe 'absolutely at the height of their powers' as they performed to enthusiastic audiences. The *Dancing Times* also noted that the opening (and by now traditional) gala in aid of the student scholarship fund

Lauren Potter in Robert Cohan's Agora *(1984)*

Patrick Harding-Irmer in
Robert Cohan's Skyward *(1984)*

OPPOSITE: Brenda Edwards in
Rite Electrik *by Tom Jobe*
(1984)

was sponsored by the Bankers Trust Company who bought nearly 500 seats in the Dress Circle and far from proving a stuffy sponsorship audience proved a highly appreciative one (how these scholarship galas have grown – just as has the Contemporary Dance Trust and all its activities! Time was when we all paid £5.00 a head for an evening at The Place, but now they attract not only royal presences but really important sponsorship. It is but one of the thrilling achievements of the London Contemporary Dance Theatre and its School that it should now attract the same kind of sponsorship as do the more obviously glamorous ballet companies.)

During the course of the evening Robin Howard was able proudly to report not only the growth of the company and the School but its world wide reputation. The School now feeds not only the LCDT but has infiltrated the USA where dancers are working with Paul Taylor, Twyla Tharp and (a high proportion) the Martha Graham company. But the plea is always the same: if these standards are to be maintained let alone raised then a 'lot more money' is needed. In addition to sending dancers to companies overseas, the company itself shared the Olympic festivities with the Royal Opera and the Royal Shakespeare companies and there are hopes now for a visit to Russia. And all this in less than 20 years.

Robin Howard's appeals for funds might seem a recurrent theme during the 1980s but as the decade wore on the starvation diet of state funding and the ever-present problems of attracting commercial sponsorship was to cast a long shadow over the company's future. The company worked in a constant climate of financial stringency and there was no gainsaying the fact that LCDT's needs were 'great and urgent' as Robin Howard wrote in the year's report:

Our main sources of income are Arts Council and Local Authority grants and box office. It had seemed that the Government and the Arts Council had accepted the exceptional needs and deserts of dance but, despite the virtual promises in The Glory of the Garden [a report on the financial state of the arts] it does not look as though LCDT will get a significant increase in its grant. The outlook for LCDT and for The Place Theatre is no brighter with the demise of sympathetic local authorities. Our box office income has risen dramatically over the past five years and can not now be expected to improve so rapidly. This makes our fund raising efforts in the private sector even more important than before.

Sally Estep and Kenneth Tharp in Richard Alston's Double Work *(1984). Photograph by David Buckland*

1985

◆

Despite the darkening financial prospects, the company embarked upon its 1985 spring tour of the regions and in Oxford, on 7 February, it presented the first performance of Siobhan Davies's *Bridge the Distance*. Inspired by Benjamin Britten's Third String Quartet, whose final movement is sub-titled 'La Serenissima', the choreography was concerned also with Venice – as was the design by David Buckland – and the central figure, danced by Patrick Harding-Irmer was clearly based on Thomas Mann's Aschenbach.

In April the company visited Geneva and Lausanne, and by June they were installed at Sadler's Wells for a one-week season which brought two programmes of recent work. But the company was gearing all its efforts towards a major fund raising effort, which was to be a gala at the Royal Opera House, Covent Garden, on 11 July. The event highlighted the very considerable difficulties in funding which now haunted every activity of the Trust. In a lengthy survey published in the *Financial Times*, Robin Howard was concerned with the threat to the LCDT standards of creativity and experimentation:

Because we are supposed to be a creative organisation, I dare to voice my disappointment with the company today. We have always produced a great deal of good new work, and we are now hindered in doing that by external circumstance rather than any glaring fault of our own.

The problem is two-fold. First, had we more money, we could allow the talent in our organisation to make the greater contribution it could give to the dance theatre in Britain and to our own company. Second, the traditional way in which touring has developed within the Arts Council's strategy inhibits creativity – we have to spend so much of our year on the road that we have neither the time nor the breathing space to produce the new work which is one of our chief claims to importance.

Without this creativity I do not believe we are justified in existing. If we fall into the same pattern as ballet companies, touring an established and safe traditional repertory, we deserve to die. There is no long-standing repertory which it is our task to show the regions. We exist simply to produce new and, we hope, valid work, with occasional outstanding pieces from elsewhere by which we may judge our attainment and the public may assess our capabilities on a broader scale.

We cannot do this now. Where previously we had time and money to mount eight or more creations in a year, we now concentrate on four. Our four

Celia Hulton and Michael Small in Shadows in the Sun *by Christopher Bannerman (1985)*

resident choreographers, headed by Robert Cohan and Siobhan Davies, should be making more new pieces. We cannot give Bob Cohan, whose immense abilities made the company and school, the breathing space his gifts merit. Choreographers in other companies can have months in which to prepare new work; Bob has half a day for six weeks, if he is lucky, during which time he is also teaching, attending committee meetings, advising all and sundry who make demands upon his time. We cannot give him the life that is essential if he is to remain the choreographer he has proved he truly is under easier circumstances.

The tensions which result from financial stringencies and unyielding arts policies are reflected in the way our company is obliged to work. Bob Cohan has built a magnificent instrument, in company and school, which our choreographers are unable at present to use to the full. We need an extra £250,000 each year in addition to our grants of £500,000 and our box office receipts, to allow us to relieve pressure and realise what should be our potential. When Bob Cohan and I started, we sought to ensure equal emphasis upon the quality of what we produced, and on the way in which we produced it. Through lack of funds we may lose something of both these qualities.

I want our school and company, and our Place Theatre, to remain a beacon for ways of dancing and ways of creating dances. Yet we effectively face worse and worse cuts in our government grants. Nearly everyone in our organisation, as in many other state-funded groups, has been underpaid for years. We are fighting to find the money that the Government says is waiting for us in the industrial and private sectors. . . .

There is not the money available in the private sector in Britain that is needed for all the arts. We are not as rich a nation as the U.S. or West Germany, which are the two chief examples given to us. We do not have a tax structure which will allow individuals to give us money as they do in America. Although industry's profitability is improving in Britain it still does not match that in America. More especially, we have a different social attitude to the arts from that in America, and there is the added fact that, if we expect the arts to receive money from commercial sources, it will be the great national and royal institutions which attract the lion's share of funding. The recent benefaction of £50m to the National Gallery is a miracle. It would be an even greater miracle were some smaller gallery, doing important work in a new way, to attract even one hundredth part of that sum.

The same is true of the performing arts. LCDT is now a national company and, as research shows, attracts a large and often affluent audience who readily respond to our more adventurous works. Furthermore, it is the backers of successful creations who will be remembered and acclaimed. Yet industry often seems happier to support something safer and more obviously accepted, like a new production of a standard classic at a long-established national or royal house.

We have, in a sense, already attained the status of an establishment organisation, but we exist to bridge a gap between the establishment and a public which does not fit into that category. We are risk-takers. If we play safe we are untrue to ourselves. We now do not have sufficient funds to venture into the unknown, which is what we should do and have done so well in the past. A short-term solution to our problem is to play safe. If we do so, we shall die. And deserve to die, because people will eventually become bored.

Above all, we shall die because we only exist through the commitment of underpaid artists, technicians and administrators, and the time will come when morale will decline because of this fact. Without wishing to seem too personal I would also make the point that I, like many other people in organisations such as ours, have been forced into an unsatisfactory and inefficient way of working. Whilst administration and fund-raising are very important aspects of duties, no less important is the need for me to help encourage and motivate our creative team. Yet desk-work and fund-raising of a kind I cannot delegate are steadily increasing at the expense of the rest. . . .

I do not want to give the impression we *shall* succumb. We are well into a development – not just a survival – plan . . . But let nobody be deceived. What companies like ourselves are fighting for is survival. We shall always do our best, and strive for the best. We hope that this will earn us the support of everyone concerned with the quality of life and art in this country.

The Royal Gala, in the presence of Prince Andrew, was a very jolly occasion. It was introduced by Natalia Makarova, the Alvin Ailey American Dance Theatre flew in to dance Billy Wilson's *Concerto in F*, and Michael Holman's New York City Breakers spun and hip-hopped on the sacred boards of the Opera House. Linda Gibbs, Christopher Bannerman and Ross McKim were seen in three solos by Kenneth MacMillan, and then Zizi Jeanmaire danced 'cheek to cheek' with Luigi Bonino in an excerpt from her husband Roland Petit's *Hollywood Paradise*. The evening came to an end with LCDT's by now traditional applause-rousing *Class*.

The gala was a huge success, not only in raising an appreciable sum for LCDT's coffers, but more especially in appealing to an audience among whom it was hoped there would be many new sponsors. With these Royal junketings over, LCDT returned to its proper task of creating dance, with a series of workshops in the following week. These had been the result of a four-week period of choreographic study and they produced eleven dances by members of the company – not for professional showing, but an important assertion of the company's undiminished drive towards new work.

After the summer holidays the annual pattern re-established itself with a return to the regions and the creation, on 24 September in Nottingham, of Christopher Bannerman's *Shadows in the Sun*. The work had been commissioned as part of the celebrations to mark the centenary of the birth of D. H. Lawrence and,

using some evocative music by Frank Bridge, Bannerman produced dances which explored attitudes he discerned in Lawrence's writings. A further acquisition in this week was Jerome Robbins' *Moves*, a work danced in silence and dating from 1959, to which LCDT's dancers gave entirely idiomatic performance.

There followed a visit to Athens in November under the auspices of the British Council and on the company's return, an historic performance took place in the nave of Canterbury Cathedral. Three years after the inception of the BA in Contemporary Dance, the first graduates were due to emerge and to mark this the company, the University of Kent at Canterbury, and the Cathedral itself combined in a service of dance and worship. Students from the school were joined by members of the company and most notably by Anca Frankenhaeuser, Patrick Harding-Irmer and Charlotte Kirkpatrick, who were among the first graduates of the honours degree course and had, be it admiringly noted, all gained first class honours. In the gathering autumnal dusk, the Cathedral glowed with light and the dancers, especially in Cohan's *Stabat Mater*, looked extraordinarily beautiful against the magnificent backdrop of the Cathedral itself. The other two works were also on religious themes, namely Pablo Ventura's *Chiaro Oscuro*, set to Weelkes's *Give Ear, O Lord*, and Robert North's *The Annunciation*.

The winter season at Sadler's Wells ran from 3 December to 21 December and brought to London the autumn's two new works, *Moves* and *Shadows in the Sun*, in a varied repertory. It also prompted Robin Howard to make clear to his audience the extreme financial problems and the threat to the company's identity which he had earlier outlined in the *Financial Times* before the Royal Gala:

> We have considered three possible policies for the future. First, there could be further belt-tightening in all areas; we have rejected this 'austerity route' because it would almost inevitably lead to a decline in creativity and a lowering of standards in our organisation. Second, important future projects could be abandoned entirely; we are unwilling to pursue such retrenchment because it will make nonsense of our entire creative policy and lead to the redundancy of vital employees. Third, we can choose 'the route of risk', quite simply because we prefer to die true to ourselves, doing what we believe in, rather than submit to slow, creative strangulation.
>
> Our Development Plan for all of Contemporary Dance Trust will follow this 'route of risk'. In terms of London Contemporary Dance Theatre, this means in essence that we will trust our artists and our audiences. . .

Patrick Harding-Irmer in Siobhan Davies's Bridge the Distance *(1985). Photograph by Bill Cooper*

1986

Nineteen eighty-six followed the usual pattern of new creations aired during the spring regional tour followed by workshops, then foreign travel, a fresh creative period culminating in a season at Sadler's Wells.

As the company approached the year of its majority it was disheartening to see how so distinguished a history of achievement should still be darkened by the ever-present problems of funding. Nevertheless, the eagerness to provide evidence of the company's creative drive – the fact that as a 'contemporary' company it had to go on making new works – was seen in the first weeks of the year when creations by Robert Cohan and Siobhan Davies were given their first performance in Eastbourne. Siobhan Davies's *The Run to Earth* was a work which explored the emotional and physical attitudes implicit in the title. Robert Cohan's *Ceremony, Slow Dance on a Burial Ground* took its tone from the score by Stephen Montague, which provided the sub-title, and also from Cohan's memories of a Peruvian burial ground where the bodies reappeared from the cracked and dried earth. The other aspects of the Trust's activities were marked by residencies in Doncaster and by workshops at The Place which found five novelties produced by members of the company.

Further innovations of the year were announced by LCDT's first collaboration with the Birmingham Hippodrome (already the second home of Sadler's Wells Royal Ballet) and the BAI Studios from 12–17 May. During this week Robert Cohan directed a programme of afternoon lecture demonstrations and open choreographic sessions. Morning sessions consisted of LCDT dancers and musicians working with a group of students selected from the local community for their commitment to contemporary dance and their past experience of LCDT's Educational Programme. The works created in these sessions were presented in the informal showing on 17 May, primarily for friends and relations of the students involved 'but interested teachers and community workers are welcome at 50p per head.' The residency closed with an open forum in which professionals from all aspects of LCDT's work talked to young people about the variety of career options which exist in dance theatre. This session was free.

In the following month the company gave its first performance in a tent, appearing in Norfolk Park, Sheffield, in The Big Top, a former circus tent which had been used for several years by the Royal Ballet, Sadler's Wells Royal Ballet and Ballet Rambert. The Big Top provided a superbly broad stage and the opportunity for a large and sometimes new public to see dance performances at modest

Anca Frankenhaeuser and Peter Dunleavy in Robert Cohan's Video Life *(1986)*

Charlotte Kirkpatrick with members of the cast of Robert Cohan's Ceremony *(1986)*

prices. For London Contemporary Dance, it represented yet another way of taking their repertory to a fresh audience.

The summer's travels took the company to Tivoli Gardens in Copenhagen and then, in August, to Italy, where Cohan had been invited to create a new work for the organisation 'Meeting for Friendship Among Peoples'. This was to be *Video Life*, which commented on the brutalising effect upon mankind of exposure to violence on television. Television screens by the side of the stage played news clips of appalling civil and military strife while on stage the LCDT artists were caught up in choreography which examined the gradual breakdown of social decency and the fabric of life.

Returned to Britain after holidays, the company was seen in Edinburgh, where two further works were premiered at the King's Theatre on 24 September. Christopher Bannerman's *Unfolding Field* was a danced salute to Halley's Comet, and Robert Cohan's *Interrogations* a highly dramatic response to Hamlet's 'To be or not to be' soliloquy. Against a complicated set by Antonio Lagarto of huge panels of sheet metal, the audience was shown a dream sequence in which images from the soliloquy whirled in surreal fashion round the figure of Darshan Singh Bhuller as Hamlet. As was customary, the year's new works were to feature in the Sadler's Wells season which ran from 18 November to 6 December and for this season Siobhan Davies provided one brand new work, *and do they do*, inspired by the warm colours of the South of France and paintings by Matisse and Picasso – the title being taken from some Gertrude Stein writing about Picasso (hence the lower case). The piece was energetically danced to a minimalist score by Michael Nyman.

Charlotte Kirkpatrick and Julian Moss in Unfolding Field *by Christopher Bannerman (1986)*

184

Towards the end of the year it was announced that Siobhan Davies had been awarded one of the prestigious Fulbright Fellowships to enable her to work in the United States. It was the first time a Fulbright had been given to a choreographer and the $15,000 award enabled Siobhan Davies and her family to spend nine months of 1987 studying in America.

As soon as the Wells season was over the company prepared to take off for a visit to Rome, performing there in the week immediately before Christmas.

Patrick Harding-Irmer and Darshan Singh Bhuller in Robert Cohan's Interrogations *(1986). Photograph by Dee Conway*

1987

◆

With the 1987 season LCDT entered on its majority. Pausing at this moment to survey the events of the past twenty-one years, what became clear was the stature of the achievement, the extraordinary nature of what had been attained through selfless endeavour. It is no exaggeration to say that the Contemporary Dance Trust, as umbrella for a school, a teaching system, a performing troupe, a manner of creativity, had altered the way a nation thought about dance – and had extended its influence into Europe.

'Dance' had not only been made respectable in the eyes of the public who had reacted so uncomprehendingly to the Graham season of 1954 (which had sparked off the Robin Howard enterprise), 'dance' had become a major fact in the experience of young people in schools and colleges, a significant force in the theatre – even, for some young people, a means of transcending the bitter fact of their social and economic situation. That these exceptional changes had been wrought in the fabric of a whole community and, indeed, of a nation, is owed directly to the work of the Contemporary Dance Trust. That within the space of the Trust's twenty-one years so much had been done, is owed to the vision of Robin Howard and Robert Cohan, and to what must be seen as the moral force that guides everything the Trust, its school and its company do.

That the collaborators have worked so long together and have been blessed with such loyalty from their associates is testimony to this fact. That audiences, of all kinds, in many cities in Britain and around the world, have reacted with such positive admiration and affection for the company – which for the general public is the outward and visible manifestation of the Trust – is further testimony to the rightness (in every sense of the word) of what the Trust has done. The expansion of dance in Britain, the many small companies who venture, with varying degrees of success and of braveness, into the sea of dance, owe their very existence to the example and to the pioneering work of the Contemporary Dance Trust and its company. The future of dance in Britain must inevitably appear still shadowed with financial uncertainties, but one thing is sure. The example of the Trust, the work of LCDT and its school, is a beacon for the future and an example for the future to emulate. Robin Howard, in his After-word, discusses some of the great possibilities envisaged for the future. In the light of what LCDT has given Britain so far, it is incumbent upon the nation to make sure these hopes are realised. Contemporary Dance is now a glorious part of our artistic history, which touches the lives of a great many people. It must continue to expand, and enhance the life of the nation.

Michael Small, Kenneth Tharp, Julian Moss and Peter Dunleavy in Daniel Ezralow's Irma Vep *(1987). Photograph by Bill Cooper*

Members of London Contemporary Dance Theatre in Siobhan Davies's Red Steps *(1987). Photograph by David Buckland*

AFTERWORD

by Robin Howard

Nineteen-eighty-seven saw the start of Contemporary Dance Trust's twenty-first anniversary year. I do not hesitate to say that until 1976, I loved every minute of my work for the Trust. Since that date, I have increasingly disliked the way in which I have had to spend my time. My one continuing joy has been the dedication of all – well, nearly all – the people with whom I have worked, despite them being badly underpaid, and the spirit of the students.

Our 21st Anniversary celebrations had three purposes: to show the breadth of our work, to secure a firm financial base for the future, and then to break out of our financial shackles and concentrate upon doing what we most believe in.

We have specific plans for the future, but these are subject to change. What must not change are our principles: to seek to serve by identifying needs and trying to satisfy them, always aiming at the highest standards and paying as much attention to how we work as to what we do. I think that we have, in a sense, to return once again to our beginnings. We have to find the means to help our new choreographers to work in such a way that they will shape the future of the company for the next twenty-one years. We have to continue to reach out to young people in many ways: by educating them through the experience of our residencies and lecture demonstrations; by educating them more directly in our School; by consideration of that education so that we may ask ourselves 'What will the dancer and choreographer in the year 2000 most benefit from, that we can give them today?' By searching into these needs and these hopes, we can help secure our choreographic and dance future, and we can help form artists whose work is the fruit of 'happy' creativity, of understanding sprung from a balance of body, mind and spirit, of wholeness in keeping with the New Age.

We have to enter upon a regenerative process, returning to our first base, but sustained by the achievements of the past twenty-one years. We must regroup our forces for another journey of exploration and development in dance. If we can do that – if funds are available – then I know that this second stage will be even more exciting than our beginnings. Without funding, we can only attain something temporary and cosmetic, but from a secure financial position we can move forward and do great things. I think I know the direction we should take, and I can start the new development. Other people will come along and take over, and guide the Trust, its School, its company, its work, into the twenty-first century. That way lies a glorious future for us.

Repertoire

AGORA (1984)

Choreography:	Robert Cohan
Music:	J. S. Bach, Brandenburg Concerto No 6 and Chaconne in D Minor for Unaccompanied Violin
Design:	Norberto Chiesa
Lighting:	Mark Henderson
Costumes made by	Annie Guyon
World premiere:	16 February 1984, Grand Theatre, Leeds (under the working title of *Common Land*)

AND THEY DO (1986)

Choreography:	Siobhan Davies
Music:	Michael Nyman
Design:	David Buckland
Lighting:	Peter Mumford
World premiere:	25 November 1986, Sadler's Wells, London

THE ANNUNCIATION (1979)

Choreography:	Robert North
Music:	Howard Blake
Lighting:	John B. Read
World premiere:	7 August 1979, Jerusalem

BEYOND THE LAW (1981)

Choreography:	Darshan Singh Bhuller
Music:	Jon Keliehor
Lighting:	Tom Johnson
World premiere:	13 May 1981, The Place

ASPECT (1981)

Choreography:	Patrick Harding-Irmer
Music:	Caroline Thompson Electronic treatment by Barrington Pheloung and Andrew Webster
Lighting:	Tom Johnson
World premiere:	6 May 1981, The Place

BLUE SCHUBERT FRAGMENTS (1974)

Choreography:	Richard Alston
Music:	Franz Schubert, 'Death and the Maiden', Song Opus 7, No 3 – Theme from the String Quartet in D Minor Also played on harmonium and flute
Lighting:	Michael Alston
Premiere:	26 February 1974, Shaw Theatre, London
World premiere:	28 August 1973, The Place First entitled *Layout*

BOX (1978)

Choreography:	Micha Bergese
Music:	'Take That' by William Albright
Lighting:	John B. Read
World premiere:	May 1978, The Place

BRIAN (1972)

Choreography:	Robert North
Music:	Michael Finnissy – additional lute music played by Julian Bream (tape), words by John Dodson (tape, live)
Design/costumes:	Peter Owen
Slide photography:	Sally Potter
Lighting:	Ian Irving
World premiere:	12 October 1972, Theatre Royal, Bath

BRIDGE THE DISTANCE (1985)

Choreography:	Siobhan Davies
Music:	Benjamin Britten, Third String Quartet
Set and costume design:	David Buckland
Frontcloth painted by	David Buckland and Peter Morgan
Lighting design:	Peter Mumford
Costumes made by	Cheryl Pike
World premiere:	7 February 1985, Apollo Theatre, Oxford

THE BRONZE (1975)

Choreography:	Namron
Music:	Bob Downes, played by the composer. Marimba, tenor saxophone & voices
Design:	Tina Bergese
Lighting:	Charter
World premiere:	15 January 1976, Hull

THE BROOD (1967)

Choreography:	Richard Kuch
Music collage:	Pierre Henry
Costumes after a design by	François Barbeau
Lighting:	Mark Brunet
LCDT premiere:	4 February 1982, Northcott Theatre, Exeter

THE CALM (1974)

Choreography:	Siobhan Davies
Music:	Geoffrey Burgon
Lighting:	Charter
World premiere:	26 September 1974, Royal Northern College of Music, Manchester

CANSO TROBAR (1983)

Choreography:	Christopher Bannerman
Music:	Based on arrangements by Martin Best and realised by Barrington Pheloung
Design:	Antony McDonald
Costumes made by	Diane Belli, Annie Guyon
Lighting:	Mark Henderson
World premiere:	20 October 1983, Warwick Arts Centre

CANTABILE (1970)

Choreography:	Noemi Lapzeson
Music:	Michael Finnissy
Design:	Peter Farmer
Lighting:	John B. Read
World premiere:	30 December 1970, The Place

CARNIVAL (1982)

Choreography:	Siobhan Davies
Music:	'Carnival of the Animals' by Saint-Saens
Design:	David Buckland and Antony McDonald
Lighting design:	Peter Mumford
World premiere:	1982, by Second Stride

CELL (1969)

Choreography:	Robert Cohan
Music:	Ronald Lloyd
Design:	Norberto Chiesa
Costumes:	Charter
Lighting:	John B. Read
World premiere:	11 September 1969, The Place

CEREMONY: Slow Dance on a Burial Ground (1986)

Choreography:	Robert Cohan
Music:	Stephen Montague 'Slow Dance on a Burial Ground'
Set Design:	Norberto Chiesa
Lighting:	Charter
Costumes painted by	Audre Gie
World premiere:	14 February 1986, Congress Theatre, Eastbourne

CHAMBER DANCES (1982)

Choreography:	Robert Cohan
Music:	Geoffrey Burgon
Costumes:	Norberto Chiesa
Lighting:	John B. Read
World premiere:	16 September 1982, Gaumont Theatre, Southampton

CHANGING YOUR MIND (1972)

Choreography:	Dan Waggoner
Speaker:	Paula Lansley
Lighting:	Charter
LCDT premiere:	26 September 1974, Royal Northern College of Music, Manchester

CLASS (1975)

Choreography:	Robert Cohan
Music:	Jon Keliehor
Design:	Charter
Lighting:	John B. Read
World premiere:	4 June 1975, The Place

COLD (1972)

Choreography:	Richard Alston
Music:	Adolphe Adam, from *Giselle* Act 2
Lighting:	John B. Read
World premiere:	1 February 1972, The Place

CONSOLATION OF THE RISING MOON (1971)

Choreography:	Robert Cohan
Music:	arr. by John Williams
Design and costumes:	Peter Farmer
World premiere:	13 January 1971, The Place

CONTINUUM (1977)

Choreography:	Micha Bergese
Music:	Morris Pert
Design:	Norberto Chiesa
Lighting:	John B. Read
World premiere:	3 September 1977, Eden Court, Inverness

DA CAPO AL FINE (1975)

Choreography:	Micha Bergese
Music:	Dominic Muldowney
Design:	Bettina Bergese
Lighting:	Charter
Costumes made by	Diana Belli
World premiere:	15 November 1975, Sadler's Wells, London
	(This work was choreographed at the First Gulbenkian Choreographic Summer School in August, 1975)

DANCE FOR FOUR (1979)

Choreography:	Tom Jobe
Music:	Bach, Violin Sonata No. 1 in G Minor
Lighting:	Charter
World premiere:	22 May, Sadler's Wells, London

DANCES OF LOVE AND DEATH (1981)

Choreography:	Robert Cohan
Music:	Carl Davis
Player Piano Music:	Conlon Nancarrow
Design:	Norberto Chiesa
Lighting design:	John B. Read
World premiere:	31 August 1981, Edinburgh Festival

THE DANCING DEPARTMENT (1983)

Choreography:	Siobhan Davies
Music:	'Musical Offering' by J. S. Bach/ Realisation by Barrington Pheloung
Design and Photography:	David Buckland
Lighting:	Peter Mumford
World premiere:	8 February 1983, Apollo Theatre, Oxford

DANGER, WORK IN PROGRESS (1981)

Producer:	Christopher Bannerman
Assisted by	Jane Kavanagh and Charlie Peacock
Music:	Erik Satie Gnossiennes; Mozart Adagio and Allegro from Sonata in F Major, K332; Stevie Wonder

	'Inner Visions', Glenn Miller 'In the Mood'; Richard Attree, Eleanor Alberga, Traditional Folk Music
Lighting:	Mark Brunet
Choreography:	Christopher Bannerman, Eleanor Alberga, Philip Taylor, Darshan Singh Bhuller
World premiere:	13 May 1981, The Place

DAYS UNTOLD (1979)

Choreography:	Patrick Harding-Irmer
Music:	Joanne Pooley
Lighting:	Charter
World premiere:	2 May, Sadler's Wells, London

DEATH AND THE MAIDEN (1980)

Choreography:	Robert North
Music:	Schubert, Death and the Maiden, 1st and 2nd movements
Lighting:	Adrian Dightam
World premiere:	12 February, 1980, Northcott Theatre, Exeter

DIARY 2: Early mornings March to June 1975 (1975)

Choreography:	Siobhan Davies
Music:	Morris Pert
Lighting:	Charter
World premiere:	6 October 1975, Royal Court, Liverpool

DIVERSION OF ANGELS (1948)

Choreography:	Martha Graham
Music:	Norman Dello Joio
Lighting:	Jean Rosenthal

World premiere by Martha Graham Company, 1948 Connecticut LCDT first performance February 1974, Nuffield Theatre, Southampton

DOUBLEWORK (1978)

Choreography:	Richard Alston
Music:	James Fulkerson
Costume design:	Jenny Henry
Lighting design:	Peter Mumford

First performed by Richard Alston and Dancers in 1978
Reconstructed for Second Stride with music by James Fulkerson

LCDT premiere:	27 November 1984, Sadler's Wells, London

DREAMS WITH SILENCES (1978)

Choreography:	Robert North
Music:	Brahms
Design:	Norberto Chiesa
Lighting:	John B. Read
World premiere:	5 October 1978, Pavilion Theatre, Bournemouth

DRESSED TO KILL (1974)

Choreography:	Robert North
Music:	Harry Miller and Dennis Smith
Designs and costumes:	Peter Farmer
World premiere:	7 February 1974, The Nuffield Theatre, Southampton

DUET (1964)

Choreography:	Paul Taylor
Music:	Joseph Haydn, Largo, Opus 51
Costumes:	George Tacit
LCDT premiere:	4 June 1970, The Place

ECLIPSE (1959)

Choreography:	Robert Cohan
Music:	Eugene Lester
Design:	Charter
Lighting:	John B. Read
British premiere:	10 October 1967, The Adeline Genée Theatre, East Grinstead

EL PENITENTE (1969)

Choreography:	Martha Graham
Music:	Louis Horst
Setting and props:	Isamu Noguchi
Lighting:	Jean Rosenthal
Set reproduced by:	Peter Donohoe
LCDT premiere:	2 September 1969, The Place

EOS (1978)

Choreography:	Robert Cohan
Music:	Barry Guy
Design:	Barney Wan
Lighting:	John B. Read
World premiere:	3 October 1978, Pavilion Theatre, Bournemouth

ESPLANADE (1975)

Choreography:	Paul Taylor
Reconstructed by:	Eileen Cropley
Music:	J. S. Bach, Violin Concerti in E Major and D Minor (Largo & Allegro)

Costumes:	John Rawlings
Lighting:	Jennifer Tipton
First performed by Paul Taylor Dance Company	
LCDT premiere:	14 September 1982, Gaumont Theatre, Southampton

FIELD (1980)

Choreography:	Robert Cohan
Music:	Brian Hodgson
Design:	Charter and Penny King
Lighting:	Charter
World premiere:	12 February 1980, Arts Centre, Christ's Hospital, Horsham

FOREST (1977)

Choreography:	Robert Cohan
Sound:	Brian Hodgson
Design:	Norberto Chiesa
Lighting:	Charter
World premiere:	12 April 1977, Sadler's Wells, London

FREE SETTING (1981)

Choreography:	Siobhan Davies
Music:	Michael Finnissy
Design and Photography:	David Buckland
Lighting:	Peter Mumford
World premiere:	15 October 1981, Arts Centre, University of Warwick

HARMONICA BREAKDOWN (1938)

Choreography:	Jane Dudley
Music:	Based on Sonny Terry
LCDT premiere:	12 April 1977, Sadler's Wells, London

HEADLONG (1973)

Choreography:	Richard Alston
Music:	Anna Lockwood
Lighting:	Charles Paton
London premiere:	15 November 1975, Sadler's Wells, London

HINTERLAND (1975)

Choreography:	Micha Bergese
Music:	Kraftwerk, Golden Seven, Andrew Sisters, Whispering Jack Smith
Design:	Bettina Bergese
Lighting:	Charter
World premiere:	18 February 1975, Shaw Theatre, London

THE HOMERUN (1981)

Choreography: Philip Taylor
Music: Christopher Benstead, 'Highland Fling'
Tape collage: Philip Taylor and Charlie Peacock
Design: Philip Taylor
Lighting: Tom Johnson
World premiere: 13 May 1981, The Place

HUNTER OF ANGELS (1967)

Choreography: Robert Cohan
Music: Bruno Maderna
Costumes: Walter Martin
Lighting: John B. Read
British premiere: 12 October 1967, The Adeline Genée Theatre, East Grinstead

ICE (1978)

Choreography: Robert Cohan
Music: Morton Subotnick
Design: Norberto Chiesa
Lighting: John B. Read
World premiere: 5 December 1978, Sadler's Wells, London

INTERROGATIONS (1986)

Choreography: Robert Cohan
Music: Barrington Pheloung
Set and costumes: Antonio Lagarto
Lighting: John B. Read
Costumes made by Cheryl Pike & Penny King
World premiere: Kings Theatre, Edinburgh

JUST BEFORE (1978)

Choreography: Anthony van Laast
Music: Organised by Anthony van Laast
Design: Angela Hawkins
Lighting: Charter
World premiere: May 1978, The Place, London

KHAMSIN (1976)

Choreography: Robert Cohan
Music: Bob Downes
Design: Norberto Chiesa
Lighting: Charter
World premiere: 22 March 1976, The Playhouse, Leeds

KISSES REMEMBERED

Choreography: Cathy Lewis
Music: Carl Vine
Design: Stuart MacLaine
Lighting: Charter

World premiere: 29 May 1979, Sadler's Wells, London

LAYOUT (1973)
See BLUE SCHUBERT FRAGMENTS (1974)

LIQUID ASSETS (1982)

Choreography: Tom Jobe
Music: Conlon Nancarrow
Lighting: Tom Johnson
World premiere: 2 August 1982, The Place

MASQUE OF SEPARATION (1975)

Choreography: Robert Cohan
Music: Burt Alcantara
Design & costumes: Norberto Chiesa
Lighting: John B. Read
World premiere: 20 February 1975, Shaw Theatre, London

MASS (1973)

Choreography: Robert Cohan
Music: Judith Wier
Design: Norberto Chiesa
Lighting: John B. Read
World premiere: 3 April 1973, The Oxford Playhouse

MEETING AND PARTING (1977)

Choreography: Robert North
Music: Howard Blake
Design: Peter Farmer
Lighting: David Hersey
World premiere: 7 April 1977, Sadler's Wells, London

MOVES

Choreography: Jerome Robbins
Staged by Tom Abbott
Lighting design: Jennifer Tipton
MOVES was created by Jerome Robbins' Ballets: USA and had its world premiere at the Festival of Two Worlds in Spoleto, Italy 1959.
LCDT premiere: 24 September 1985, Theatre Royal, Nottingham

NEMA (1976)

Choreography: Micha Bergese
Music: Eberhard Schoener
Design: Bettina Bergese
Lighting: David Hersey
World premiere: 4 November 1976, Royal Northern College of Music, Manchester

NEW GALILEO (1984)

Choreography:	Siobhan Davies
Music:	John Adams, 'Phrygian Gates'
Design and lighting design	David Buckland and Peter Mumford
World premiere:	14 February 1984, The Grand, Leeds

NIGHT WATCH (1977)

Choreography:	Micha Bergese, Robert Cohan, Siobhan Davies, Robert North
Music:	Bob Downes
Design:	Norberto Chiesa
Lighting:	Charter
World premiere:	5 April 1977, Sadler's Wells, London

NO MAN'S LAND (1974)

Choreography:	Robert Cohan
Music:	Barry Guy, 'Statements 11' for double bass
Design:	Peter Farmer
Costumes made by	Adele Thompson
Lighting:	Richard Caswell
World premiere:	13 November 1974, Sadler's Wells, London

NOWHERE SLOWLY (1971)

Choreography:	Richard Alston
Music:	Terry Riley, 'Poppy Nogood & the Phantom Band'
Lighting:	Nora Stapleton
World premiere:	6 January 1971, The Place

NYMPHEAS (1976)

Choreography:	Robert Cohan
Music:	Debussy
	1st Arabesque
	3 Preludes – Feuilles Mortes, Les Fées sont d'exquises danseuses, Bruyères
	Claire de lune (from Suite Bergamasque)
	La plus que lente
	Pagodes (from Suite Estampes)
Design:	Norberto Chiesa
Lighting:	John B. Read
World premiere:	22 June 1976, Theatre Royal, York (York Festival)

ONE (1980)

Choreography:	Tom Jobe
Music:	Bernie Holland
Lyrics:	Tom Jobe and Patti Jobe
Design:	Derek Jarman
Lighting:	Charter
World premiere:	12 February 1980, Arts Centre, Christ's Hospital, Horsham

ONE WAS THE OTHER (1972)

Choreography:	Noemi Lapzeson and Robert North
Music:	Arranged by Michael Finnissy
	Tape sections by Bob Downes
Design:	Norberto Chiesa
Lighting:	John B. Read
World premiere:	27 January 1972, The Place

PEOPLE ALONE (1972)

Choreography:	Robert Cohan
Music:	Bob Downes
Set Design:	Norberto Chiesa
Costumes:	Jane Hyland and Norberto Chiesa
Lighting:	John B. Read
World premiere:	29 August 1972, The Place

PEOPLE TOGETHER (1973)

Choreography:	Robert Cohan
Music:	Bob Downes
Design:	Norberto Chiesa
Lighting:	John B. Read
Costumes:	Charter
World premiere:	26 February 1973, The Place

PILOT (1974)

Choreography:	Siobhan Davies
Music:	Igg Welthy
Lighting:	Charter
World premiere:	7 February 1974, Nuffield Theatre, Southampton

PLACE OF CHANGE (1975)

Choreography:	Robert Cohan
Music:	Schoenberg
Design:	Charter
Lighting:	John B. Read
Costumes made by:	Diana Belli
World premiere:	22 December 1975, Sadler's Wells, London

RAINBOW BANDIT (1977)

Choreography:	Richard Alston
Sound:	'Just' (1972) by Charles Amirkhanian
Lighting:	Charter
Costumes co-ordinated by:	Anne Guyon
World premiere:	8 December 1977, Sadler's Wells, London

RECALL (1981)

Choreography:	Jayne Lee
Music:	Cathy Lewis
Design:	Judy Stedman
Lighting:	Charlie Peacock
World premiere:	13 May 1981, The Place

REFLECTIONS (1976)

Choreography:	Robert North
Music:	Howard Blake
Lighting:	Charter

Originally commissioned and performed by the Ballet Rambert

LCDT premiere:	24 May 1979, Sadler's Wells, London

RITE ELECTRIK (1984)

Choreography:	Tom Jobe
Music:	Barrington Pheloung
Costume design:	Paul Dart
Set and lighting design:	Peter Mumford
World premiere:	21 September 1984, Derngate, Northampton

RUN LIKE THUNDER (1983)

Choreography:	Tom Jobe
Music:	Barrington Pheloung
Design:	Paul Dart
Lighting design	Peter Mumford
World premiere:	22 September 1983, Haymarket Theatre, Leicester

THE RUN TO EARTH (1986)

Choreography:	Siobhan Davies
Music:	Brian Eno, 'On Land'
Sound design for Brian Eno:	Yoni Cohen
Set and costume design:	David Buckland and Russell Mills
Lighting design:	Peter Mumford
Costumes made by	Cheryl Pike
World premiere:	12 February 1986, Congress Theatre, Eastbourne

SAND STEPS (1979)

Choreography:	Christopher Bannerman
Music:	Marcus West
Design:	Jenny Henry
Lighting:	Adrian Dightam
World premiere:	29 May 1979, Sadler's Wells, London

SCENE SHIFT (1979)

Choreography:	Micha Bergese
Music:	Carl Vine
Design:	Liz da Costa
Lighting:	John B. Read

World premiere:	22 May 1979, Sadler's Wells, London

SCRIABIN PRELUDES AND STUDIES (1978)

Choreography:	Robert North
Music:	Scriabin
Design:	Peter Farmer
Lighting:	Francis Reid
World premiere:	23 February 1978, Haymarket Theatre, Leicester

SECOND TURNING (1982)

Choreography:	Christopher Bannerman
Music:	Gyorgy Ligeti (Monument, Self-Portrait, Movement)
Design:	Antony McDonald
Lighting:	Charter
World premiere:	11 October 1982, Ryerson Theatre, Toronto

SHADOWS IN THE SUN (1985)

Choreography:	Christopher Bannerman
Music:	Frank Bridge
Design:	Andrew Storer
Lighting design:	Mark Henderson
Costumes made by	Philip Reynolds
World premiere:	24 September 1985, Theatre Royal, Nottingham

THE SINGING (1980)

Choreography:	Christopher Bannerman
Music:	Barrington Pheloung
Design:	Chris Francis and Ian Chisholm
Costumes devised by	Christopher Bannerman and Sharon Boughen
Lighting:	Charter
World premiere:	7 October 1980, Theatr Clwyd, Mold

SKY (1967)

Choreography:	Robert Cohan
Music:	Eugene Lester
World premiere:	10 October 1967, The Adeline Genée Theatre, East Grinstead

SKYWARD (SKYLARK) (1984)

Choreography:	Robert Cohan
Music:	Eleanor Alberga, 'Clouds'
Design:	Norberto Chiesa
Costumes made by	Annie Guyon
Lighting design:	John B. Read
World premiere:	19 September 1984, Derngate, Northampton

SOLO RIDE (1978)

Choreography:	Micha Bergese
Music:	Douglas Gould
Design:	Liz da Costa
Costumes painted by	Liz da Costa, Penny Hadkill
World premiere:	24 October 1978, Royal Northern College of Music, Manchester

SOME DANCE AND SOME DUET (1980)

Choreography:	Micha Bergese
Music:	Stravinsky
Design:	Liz da Costa
Lighting:	Adrian Dightam
World premiere:	12 February 1980, Arts Centre, Christ's Hospital, Horsham

SOMETHING TO TELL (1980)

Choreography:	Siobhan Davies
Music:	Benjamin Britten, Third cello suite; Variations on Russian Folk Songs
Design:	Antony McDonald
Lighting:	Peter Mumford
World premiere:	9 October 1980, Theatr Clwyd, Mold

SONGS AND DANCES (1981)

Choreography:	Robert North
Music:	Schubert, *Quartettsatz*; Songs
Design:	Andrew Storer
Costumes made by	Clare Mussellwite and Catherine Darcy
Lighting:	John B. Read
World premiere:	3 February 1981, Northcott Theatre, Exeter

SONGS, LAMENTATIONS AND PRAISES (1979)

Choreography:	Robert Cohan
Music:	Geoffrey Burgon
Design:	Norberto Chiesa
Lighting design:	John B. Read
World premiere:	7 August 1979, Jerusalem

SPHINX (1977)

Choreography:	Siobhan Davies
Music:	Barrington Pheloung
Lighting:	Charter
World premiere:	25 October 1977, Royal Northern College of Music, Manchester

SPINNAKER (1983)

Choreography:	Jayne Lee
Music:	Eleanor Alberga
Design:	Craig Givens
Lighting design:	Tom Johnson
World premiere:	20 September 1983, Haymarket Theatre, Leicester

STABAT MATER (1975)

Choreography:	Robert Cohan
Music:	Vivaldi
Design:	Charter
Lighting:	John B. Read
Costumes made by:	Diana Belli
World premiere:	29 September 1975, MacRobert Arts Centre, Stirling

STAGES (1971)

Production:	Robert Cohan
Music for Stage I:	Arne Nordheim
Music for Stage II:	Bob Downes
Design and costumes:	Peter Farmer
Wigs and masks:	Barbara Wilkes
Film sequences and screen projections:	Anthony McCall
Lighting:	John B. Read
World premiere:	21 April 1971, The Place

STEP AT A TIME (1976)

Choreography:	Siobhan Davies
Music:	Geoffrey Burgon
Lighting:	Charter
Photography:	Michael Creevy
World premiere:	4 November, Royal Northern College of Music, Manchester

STILL LIFE (1975)

Choreography:	Robert North
Music:	Bob Downes, Score: 'Bird of the 7th Dimension', commissioned in 1970 by Cologne Opera House, Tanz Forum, and excerpts from 'Episodes at 4 am.'
Design:	Peter Farmer
Film:	Peter Selby, John Garland, Mike Brewster
Story and co-ordination:	John Dodson, Dave Hall, Joe McAllister
Lighting:	John B. Read
World premiere:	18 February 1975, Shaw Theatre, London

THEN YOU CAN ONLY SING (1978)

Choreography:	Siobhan Davies
Music and words:	Judyth Knight
Design:	Jenny Henry
Lighting:	Charter
World premiere:	24 October 1978, Royal Northern College of Music, Manchester

THREE EPITAPHS (1956)

Choreography:	Paul Taylor
Music:	American Folk
Costumes:	Robert Rauschenberg
Lighting:	Jennifer Tipton
LCDT premiere:	28 May 1970, The Place

THREE SOLOS (1979)

Choreography:	Linda Gibbs
Music:	Dudley James
Lighting:	Adrian Dightam
World premiere:	22 May 1979, Sadler's Wells, London

THROUGH BLUE (1979)

Choreography:	Anthony van Laast
Music:	Bruce Cole
Lighting:	Charter
World premiere:	29 May 1979, Sadler's Wells, London

TIGER BALM (1972)

Choreography:	Richard Alston
Music:	'Tiger Balm' by Anna Lockwood
Lighting:	Charles Paton
World premiere:	18 December 1972, The Place

TROY GAME (1974)

Choreography:	Robert North
Music:	Batucada (Brazilian); 'Shadow Boxing Solo' by Bob Downes
Design:	Peter Farmer
Lighting:	Charter
World premiere:	3 October 1974, Royal Court Theatre, Liverpool

TZAIKERK (1976)

Choreography:	Robert Cohan
Music:	Alan Hovhaness
Lighting:	Brian Benn
World premiere:	10 October 1967, The Adeline Genée Theatre, East Grinstead

UNDER THE SAME SUN (1983)

Choreography:	Darshan Singh Bhuller
Music:	John Millar (Jhalib), Clem Alford
Costume design:	Celeste Dandeker
Lighting design:	Tom Johnson
World premiere:	20 September 1983, Haymarket Theatre, Leicester

UNFOLDING FIELD (1986)

Choreography:	Christopher Bannerman
Design:	Andrew Storer
Lighting:	Mark Henderson
Music:	Man Jumping
World premiere:	24 September 1986, Kings Theatre, Edinburgh

VESALII ICONES (1970)

Choreography:	William Louther
Music:	Peter Maxwell-Davies with the Fires of London
Lighting:	John B. Read
World premiere:	31 May 1970, The Place

VIDEO LIFE (1986)

Choreography:	Robert Cohan
Music:	Barry Guy
Design:	Norberto Chiesa
Lighting:	Charter
World premiere:	27 August 1986, Rimini, Italy

WATERLESS METHOD OF SWIMMING INSTRUCTION
or
A DAY AT THE SWIMMING POOL (1974)

Choreography:	Robert Cohan
Music:	Bob Downes
Designs and costumes:	Ian Murray Clark
Lighting:	John B. Read
World premiere:	11 June 1974, The Lausanne Festival, Switzerland

WHEN SUMMER'S BREATH (1978)

Choreography:	Micha Bergese
Music:	Michael Finnissy
Design:	Bettina Bergese
Lighting:	John B. Read
World premiere:	23 January 1978, Harrogate

INDEX